BOXING SHORTS

1,001 OF THE SPORT'S FUNNIEST ONE-LINERS

GLENN LIEBMAN

CONTEMPORARY BOOKS

A TRIBUNE NEW MEDIA/EDUCATION COMPANY

Library of Congress Cataloging-in-Publication Data

Boxing shorts : 1,001 of the sport's funniest one-liners /
   [compiled by] Glenn Liebman.
        p.   cm.
    Includes index.
    ISBN 0-8092-3216-2
    1. Boxing—Quotations, maxims, etc.
   2. Boxers (Sports)—Quotations.   I. Liebman, Glenn.
   GV1135.B69   1996
   796.8'3—dc20   95-49542
                                     CIP

Published by Contemporary Books, Inc.
Two Prudential Plaza, Chicago, Illinois 60601-6790
Manufactured in the United States of America
International Standard Book Number: 0-8092-3216-2
10   9   8   7   6   5   4   3   2   1

To my father-in-law, Bill Coll,
who has more heart and courage
than any of the great heavyweights

ACKNOWLEDGMENTS

First of all, I'd like to thank my agent, Philip Spitzer, and, of course, my wonderful editor, Nancy Crossman, the person most responsible for the Shorts series. I'd also like to thank Project Editor Craig Bolt for his professionalism and sense of humor.

I want to extend a special thanks to Ed Brophy, the Executive Director of the International Boxing Hall of Fame. In addition to being a font of information, he granted me liberal access to the Hall of Fame library, for which I am grateful.

Those of you who have read any of my other Shorts books have probably noticed that I tend to go on and on when it comes to thanking friends and family members. This time, however, I am keeping it short and to the point. I'd like to thank my brother, Bennett, one of the all-time best people in the world, for introducing me to the world of sports and for coming with me every year to the Boxing Hall of Fame. And I'd like to thank Frankie for bringing so much happiness into my life over the past year. Sleep deprivation is a small price to pay for the joy of looking into his smiling face and sharing his excitement as he explores his world. He is the greatest.

Speaking of the greatest, I'd especially like to thank Kathleen Marie for making all the good things possible. She has an amazing ability to put up with my daily obsessions about this book and my day job. Also, she doesn't complain when I try to teach Frankie how to disco. She is simply the best!

INTRODUCTION

Of the few traditions left in my life, one stands out beyond all others. Every year on the first Sunday in June, my brother, Bennett, and I drive two and a half hours to the induction ceremonies of the International Boxing Hall of Fame, located in Canastota, New York.

It is a wonderful event. The great ones are there, live and in the flesh; and, for the most part, they are incredibly approachable (which is certainly not the case at the Baseball Hall of Fame induction ceremonies). Over the years, I've had the opportunity to meet Joe Frazier, Aaron Pryor, Alexis Arguello, Don Dunphy, Bob Foster, the Spinks brothers, Ken Norton, Gene Fullmer, Angelo Dundee, Emile Griffith, Carmen Basilio, and many others.

An important aspect of our yearly pilgrimage to Canastota is that during the entire trip, my brother and I discuss only boxing—and nothing else. We talk about the great matches—Dempsey–Firpo, Louis–Conn, Louis–Schmeling, Ali–Frazier, Ali–Foreman, Graziano–Zale, Robinson–LaMotta, Hagler–Leonard, the first Pryor-Arguello fight (my all-time favorite). These memorable contests are splendid reminders of boxing's greatness.

As with my other four books, researching this book provided quite a few pleasant revelations; I was once again surprised at the amount of wit attributed to some of the all-time great boxers. We all know about Ali and Foreman, but how about former heavyweight champ Max Baer? After losing the heavyweight title to James Braddock, Baer commented, "Jim can use the title; he has five kids. I don't know how many I have." Then there are the one-liners of the man many consider the greatest of all time—Willie Pep. Responding to stories circulating about his death, Pep once remarked, "Nah, I'm not dead. I ain't even been out of the house." On the subject of death, the greatest heavyweight of them all, Joe Louis, said, "Everybody wants to go to heaven, but nobody wants to die." Another great wit was Maxie Rosenbloom, who explained why he was divorcing his psychologist wife: "After six years, I finally got a divorce. I didn't feel at home with her. My wife had so many books in the house, whenever I came in, I had to show her a library card."

Sit back, relax, and enjoy the punches and body shots of the funniest boxers of all time.

"It was all set, but like a fool, I went for a coffee break."

> *Rocky Graziano, on being told he was getting a TV commercial for a tea company*

"You talk too good."

> *Rocky Graziano, telling Sugar Ray Robinson why he could never do commercials*

"It will run as a three-minute commercial during *The Simpsons*."

> *David Letterman, on Mike Tyson's fight on Fox against Buster Mathis Jr.*

"Ali could sell the Brooklyn Bridge. Holmes couldn't sell you bread in a famine."

> *Jim Murray, contrasting the styles of Muhammad Ali and Larry Holmes*

"The man who views the world at 50 the same as he did at 20 has wasted 30 years of his life."
Muhammad Ali

"Thirty-six is getting to the age. You know it's time to leave, but something tells you you've got one more gamble."
Muhammad Ali

"Geezers at Caesars."
Anonymous, on a proposed Larry Holmes–George Foreman fight

"I wouldn't even entertain such an idea. It would be pathetic. Why would anyone pay money to see us waltzing around the ring?"
Joe Bugner, at age 44, on the idea of fighting George Foreman

"Doing nothing is treacherous."
Art Donovan, legendary ref, on staying active at age 82

"Those two guys have been around. They're as old as water."

Angelo Dundee, on Roberto Duran's cornermen, 74-year-old Fred Brown and 81-year-old Ray Arcel

"I'm fighting for every guy who ever got told to act your age."

George Foreman

"The question isn't at what age I want to retire—it's at what income."

George Foreman

"I was waiting for him to fall and he'd punch me back. Talk about sassing your elders."

George Foreman, on Axel Schulz's refusing to go down despite Foreman's best punches

"I should've fought him in the '80s."

Larry Holmes, asked what he should have done differently in fighting Holyfield in the early '90s

"I'm not like wine. I get worse with age."
>   *Larry Holmes, at age 31*

"I learned one thing. I learned not to fight when you're old."
>   *Roy Jones, on what he learned from the 43-year-old Roberto Duran's losing to Vinnie Pazienza*

"Age is like a bulldozer. It's gonna push you out of the way once you stop moving."
>   *Archie Moore*

"I don't enjoy being struck by children."
>   *Archie Moore, fighting a 29-year-old at age 44*

"My mother should know. She was there."
>   *Archie Moore, on conflicts over whether he was born in 1913 or 1916*

"I have given this a lot of thought and have decided that I must have been three when I was born."
>   *Archie Moore, on the disagreement over whether he was born in 1913 or 1916*

"I would not be surprised to hear that following Holmes, Holyfield will be holding strong negotiations with Floyd Patterson and Jersey Joe Walcott."

> *Rock Newman, on Holyfield's fighting the aging Holmes*

"Young men have vision; old men have dreams. But the place for old men to dream is beside the fire."

> *Red Smith, on the comebacks of older fighters*

"What do you think I maintain an office for—to use the bathroom down the hall?"

> *Herman Taylor, longtime promoter, on rumors that he retired in his late 80s*

ALI—FRAZIER

"This might shock and amaze ya, but I'm gonna retire Joe Frazier."

> *Muhammad Ali, before his first fight with Joe Frazier*

"I'd put Smokey Joe Frazier into orbit as the first black astronaut."

> *Muhammad Ali, before his first fight with Frazier*

"I've got two punches for Frazier—the balloon punch and the needle punch. My left jab is the balloon and the right is the needle."

> *Muhammad Ali*

"More people come to see me open a supermarket than to see Joe Frazier defend his championship."

> *Muhammad Ali*

"I don't like Joe Frazier. He talks too much. I don't like fighters who talk too much."

> *Muhammad Ali*

"It wouldn't smell good."

> *Muhammad Ali, who has a cologne named after him, on why Joe Frazier doesn't*

"Herbert [Muhammad] and I know what we want. Now you guys put it in law language."

> Yankee Durham, Frazier's manager,
> arranging the first Ali–Frazier fight

"I'm happy the guy's in my time, and I'm sure he's happy I'm in his time. He wouldn't be making the money fighting those other guys that he made fighting me."

> Joe Frazier, on Ali

AMATEURS

"I only had two fights as an amateur and lost both of them. Heck, I figure I didn't have much of a future there—so I turned pro."

> Tex Cobb

"What do you get out of fighting as an amateur? A watch, and what good is a watch? Sure, you can hock it for half of what it's worth, but that takes time and trouble. Get me a fight for dough."

> Billy Conn, on wanting to fight
> professionally

"I loved it until somebody hit me back."
> *Jackie Mason, on fighting as an amateur*

"It's boxing matches in the amateurs. It's fistfights in the pros."
> *Joe Sayatovich, Terry Norris's manager*

AMISH COUNTRY

"Tell me where he's at. I'll buy his town and have him deported."
> *Muhammad Ali, after being told about an Amish man who had never heard of him*

ANIMAL KINGDOM

"I love the opera, but I am a practical man."
> *Muhammad Ali, turning down a proposal to ride an elephant in a production of* Aïda

"Put 'em up and fight like a man."

Max Baer, while fighting in an exhibit against a real bear

"I'll tell you, boys, he's a-gonna get bitten by one big, bad Baer."

Max Baer, explaining what he was going to do to Primo Carnera when they fought

"I got to know them pretty well and we would wrestle around. They scratched and once in a while get careless with their teeth. I do not recommend wrestling with lions as part of training."

Oscar Bonavena, on training with lions

"I was so bored. I was teaching the lizards to do push-ups."

Angelo Dundee, on the postponement of the Ali–Foreman fight in Zaire

"I look like a junkyard dog. He looks like Elvis."

George Foreman, after his fight with Axel Schulz

"I guess I proved I have some dog in me—Doberman pinscher."

> *Larry Holmes, accused of being a*
> *dog before fighting Earnie Shavers*

"I reckon it's because of my unique talent for ridding my life of snakes and rodents, some of which were people."

> *Archie Moore, on how he acquired*
> *the name "Mongoose"*

"Everyone in my family's a boxer. Everybody's a boxer except one. He's my cocker spaniel."

> *Willie Pep*

"For that kind of dough, we can draw. I'd fight a lion, and they wouldn't even have to weigh him."

> *Mickey Walker, on Jimmy McLarnin's*
> *refusing to fight him because of*
> *problems with weights*

ART ARAGON

"There was nobody like Art Aragon. He was a perfect combination—showman, fighter, and rat."
Jackie McCoy, former manager

RAY ARCEL

"One of the most gentle, kind, and refined of men, he was concerned about the fighter as a person more than anyone else I ever met. To him I would have entrusted a son."
W. C. Heinz, on Ray Arcel

"Ray Arcel is the only man I've ever known who would say 'yes, ma'am' and 'no, ma'am' in a house of prostitution."
Damon Runyon

ART

"I'm the best damn artist who ever spent nine years in the fourth grade."

> *Rocky Graziano*

"I like this one because it looks like some of the guys I beat up."

> *Rocky Graziano, on a cubist work by Picasso*

"It's the only thing that could keep Mickey Walker on canvas."

> *Doc Kearns, on Walker's paintings*

"As a youth I could express myself with my fists. Physical experience belongs to youth. Then the years go by. I find art and expression in colors."

> *Mickey Walker, on his paintings*

"It looks like me. What do you want me to say, I look like Robert Redford?"

> *Chuck Wepner, on a self-portrait that hangs over his bed that his wife can't stand*

BAD PREDICTIONS

"He's gonna win the election with no problem, just like I'm gonna win my next fight."

> *Muhammad Ali, declaring a victory for Jimmy Carter in the presidential election and for himself over Larry Holmes*

"I would bet on Cooney. He may hit Larry so hard, he may join his kinfolks in Africa."

> *Muhammad Ali, predicting victory for Gerry Cooney over Larry Holmes*

"Holyfield's a courageous guy who's in great shape, but he'll take too much punishment. The refs will have to stop it. Simply a case of a big man beating a small man."

> *Angelo Dundee, predicting that Buster Douglas would beat Evander Holyfield, who knocked Douglas out in the third round*

"I have been fighting too long. I'm tired of the sport."

> *Roberto Duran, retiring from boxing*
> *in 1980 (he's still fighting today)*

"It'll either be stopped by the refs or the Red Cross."

> *Lou Duva, predicting the loss of*
> *George Foreman to Michael Moorer*

"Excuses, excuses. That's the case with Riddick Bowe. I don't think he has the character, the mental strength to beat Evander."

> *Lou Duva, before a fight in which*
> *Bowe decisioned Holyfield*

"Heavyweight champs last only two or three years. Now it's my turn."

> *George Foreman, in 1973*

"He will dance for a while and then he will start running and then I will catch him. . . . When I catch him, he will fall."

> *George Foreman, on what he would*
> *do to Ali in Zaire*

"**B**aer will knock Braddock out inside of three rounds . . . and may injure him fatally."

> *Paul Gallico, before Jim Braddock upset Max Baer to win the heavyweight title*

"**I**t's as if Joe DiMaggio's hitting streak was equaled or broken on a bunt single that somehow doesn't roll foul."

> *Richard Hoffer, Los Angeles Times, declaring that Larry Holmes's tying of Rocky Marciano's undefeated streak by beating Michael Spinks would make the new streak insignificant (Holmes lost the fight)*

"**W**hen I'm 38, I'll have better things to do than get punched—like sit at home and watch guys get punched on TV."

> *Larry Holmes, after fighting a 38-year-old Ali (at 38, Holmes fought Mike Tyson)*

"**H**e's too inexperienced to be taking on a brute like Liston."

> *Rocky Marciano, predicting that Cassius Clay would lose to Sonny Liston in their first fight*

"I looked this bum over and decided I wasn't very interested. For one thing, he wasn't very big, so I turned my back on the fellow. It was Jack Dempsey."

> *Billy McCarney, fight manager*

"I'm afraid Larry will chew him up. Michael may be faster than Larry, but you can only go so fast."

> *Archie Moore, predicting an easy win for Larry Holmes over Michael Spinks*

"Compared to him, Custer was even money."

> *Jim Murray, on Sugar Ray Leonard's chances of beating Marvin Hagler*

"About a minute and 33 seconds."

> *Ed Schuyler, AP writer, asked how long he was expected to stay in Japan for the Mike Tyson–Buster Douglas fight*

"Well, all the training I need is a haircut and a shave to beat his head off in one round."

> *John L. Sullivan, predicting an easy win over James J. Corbett (Corbett won the fight)*

"No way I can lose."

> Mike Tyson, *before facing Buster*
> *Douglas*

"I guess he can punch, but he's got two left feet. He can't box a little bit. I've never seen anybody easier to hit."

> *Jersey Joe Walcott, before facing*
> *Rocky Marciano (Marciano knocked*
> *him out in the 13th)*

"If I can't beat this bum, take my name off the record books."

> *Jersey Joe Walcott, before facing*
> *Rocky Marciano*

"Hagler, quickly. It's a mismatch. One guy hasn't fought for years and has what I consider to be a physical impairment . . . and if it isn't a physical impairment, it's a mental impairment."

> *Dick Young, sportswriter, predicting*
> *victory for Marvin Hagler over Sugar*
> *Ray Leonard*

"The man with the million-dollar body and ten-cent brain."

Anonymous, on Max Baer

"The only way you're sure he won't get into some sort of trouble is to put a chain around his neck and lead him around like a performing bear."

Jack Dempsey, on Baer

"Nobody took it like ol' Maxie Baer. Hittin' him was like knockin' a brick out of a wall."

Joe Louis

"Hey, Max, why don't you get down on the floor so the customers can recognize you?"

Jack White, owner of the cabaret where Baer did comedy routines

"You're always saying Ali isn't what he was 10 years ago, but neither are you, Howard Cosell."

> *Muhammad Ali, grabbing Cosell's toupee*

"If they cut my bald head open, they will find one boxing glove. That's all I am. I live it."

> *Marvin Hagler*

"Tommy will be looking for that big punch. Where is that bald head? Where is it? Where is it? It'll be a mirage."

> *Marvin Hagler, on how he will fight Tommy Hearns*

"It calls to mind every villain in every James Bond movie."

> *Jim Murray, on Marvin Hagler's bald head*

BASEBALL

"I could only spar with my sister, and Dad said I couldn't hit her in the face, chest, or stomach. So all she did was belt me around."

> *Judy Johnson, baseball Hall of Famer, on why he gave up boxing for baseball*

BASKETBALL

"Celebrities used to go to boxing matches. Now they're Knick fans. This may or may not be a coincidence."

> *Gil LeBreton, sportswriter, on the rough-and-tumble play of the New York Knicks*

"I'm going to get drunk for a month. Somebody give me a pocketful of money and I won't come back until I spend it."

> *Tex Cobb, on getting $100,000 for fighting Ken Norton*

"I won't know until I get sober."

> *Tex Cobb, on his career plans after fighting Larry Holmes*

"I don't run good, but I'm the happiest guy in the world."

> *Jake LaMotta, on spiking his orange juice with brandy before his morning run*

"Say all the bad things you want about alcoholism and I'll agree. Still, it was through booze that I met 2 chief justices, 50 boxing champs, 6 presidents, and my accountant."

> *Toots Shor, owner of the legendary New York City restaurant*

"I knew I was gonna be somebody. If it was a drunk, I was gonna be the best drunk that ever was."

Leon Spinks

"A stein of bourbon, and be quick about it."

John L. Sullivan, asked to name his favorite food

BIRD OF HAPPINESS

"That's lucky—lucky it wasn't me."

Freddie Brown, after a pigeon flew into the gym and pooped on Duke Stefano, who was told by Brown it was a sign of luck

THE BITTER END

"If you do, I'll never speak to you again."

Jim Braddock, after a referee told him he was going to end a fight against Joe Louis

"Did he go the distance?"

Sugar Ray Leonard, on Roberto Duran's fighting a four-round exhibition after the "No Mas" fight

"A champion has the right to choose how he goes out."

Barney Ross, pleading with a referee to allow him to come out for the final round in a fight even though he was losing badly

BLOOD LINES

"When I came back to the corner bleedin', they put some goop on the cut and said, 'Randall, don't get hit there anymore.'"

Randall "Tex" Cobb, on his tendency to bleed during fights

"Hallacy is the boxer in the green trunks and red blood."

Don Dunphy, after Mike Hallacy fought Vito Antuofermo

"I'm not scared of blood. Matter of fact, it turns me on."

Marvin Hagler

"Does Wepner have a no-cut contract?"

John Hall, Los Angeles Times *writer, on Chuck Wepner*

"Instead of a right cross, Wepner's best weapon is the Red Cross."

John Hall

"Blood is like champagne to a fighter. It gives his ego bubbly sensations."

Al Lacey, trainer

"I asked the ref, 'Why did you stop it?' He said, 'You're cut real bad under your eye.' I looked at the floor and there was a big pool of blood. I said, 'That's mine. OK.'"

Scott LeDoux, agreeing with a referee's decision to stop a fight against George Foreman

"I'm a colorful fighter. I bleed a lot."

Willie Pep

"This is just phenomenal. I think it is a little bit like a car race. There is a smell of blood in the air."

>*Ivana Trump, while attending a*
>*Spinks–Tyson match*

"He has been known to bleed when kissed on the forehead by small children."

>*Dave Anderson,* New York Times
>*sportswriter, on Chuck Wepner,*
>*known as the "Bayonne Bleeder"*

"I have three medals from the Red Cross for donating blood."

>*Chuck Wepner, on bleeding so much*

BODY SHOTS

"You're in there all alone. When you take a punch to the belly, you can't say, 'Time out!' You've got to be able to weather the storm."

>*Ray Arcel*

"The head got eyes."

> *Sam Langford, on why he punched to the body so much*

"A drop of rain will hurt you if you let enough drops hit you first."

> *Joe Louis, on Billy Conn's hitting him with a lot of jabs*

BORING BOUTS

"Watching [Tommy] Loughran and [Mike] McTigue fight is about as exciting as watching a man read a book."

> *Bill Corum, boxing writer*

"Next time, better a bout with pneumonia."

> *Peter Coutros, TV reporter, on a Renaldo Snipes–Eddie Mustafa Muhammad fight*

"The first no-hitter in the new Yankee Stadium."

> *Joe Garagiola, on the third fight between Ali and Ken Norton, which took place in Yankee Stadium*

"The Louis–Baer fight was the most disgusting public spectacle outside of a hanging that your correspondent ever witnessed."

> *Ernest Hemingway, on Joe Louis's beating Max Baer in four rounds*

"By Round 8, if someone didn't know it was for the championship of the world, if he'd just tuned in, he'd have thought it was a comedy."

> *Jimmy Jacobs, manager, on the Larry Holmes–Earnie Shavers fight*

"The fight? There was no fight."

> *Jack London, on Jack Johnson's destroying Tommy Burns*

"Leon Spinks had a no-hitter going."

> *Jim Murray, on the second Spinks–Ali fight*

"Ted Mack's Amateur Hour."

> *Rock Newman, describing a fight between Lennox Lewis and Frank Bruno*

"I started boxing because I thought it was the fastest way for black people to make it."
Muhammad Ali

"Boxing is the image of war with none of its guilt and only 25 percent of its dangers."
Anonymous

"Boxing is like sin. It's too popular to be abolished."
Dave Anderson

"This is the greatest of all sports. They don't play around with no substitutes in boxing, like they do in basketball, baseball, or football. If a boxer gets a busted rib, he stays in there with it or he is a loser."
Freddie Brown

"Boxing is a contest of will and skill, with the will generally overcoming the skill, unless the skill of one man is much greater than the skill of the other."
Cus D'Amato

"I was born to fight. I don't know what else to do."
Roberto Duran

"Boxing is the sport to which all others aspire."
George Foreman

"Boxing is like jazz. The better it is, the less people appreciate it."
George Foreman

"I just keep hitting them until they can't stand it anymore. Then they fall down."
Wilfredo Gomez, describing his boxing style

"It's a terrible sport, but it's a sport. The fight for survival is the fight."
Rocky Graziano

"The hardest thing about being a boxer is learning to pick your teeth up with your gloves on."
Kin Hubbard

"Whatever that other fellow wants to do, don't let him do it."

Sam Langford, stating his competitive philosophy

"Every major prizefight is like a morality play, a John Wayne movie, a Horatio Alger novel. There's a good guy and a bad guy."

Jim Murray

"Boxing is the best and most individual lifestyle you can have in society without being a criminal."

Randy Neumann

"Once you get in the door in boxing, you're on your own. Boxing is like nothing else. They'll knock you flat on your back."

Ferdie Pacheco, asked if Marvis Frazier had an advantage from being Joe's son

"It will be a great life. The food was good and the hours were short."

Willie Pep, on his career

"What you got to realize is that fighting is just the game that we play."

Michael Spinks, after Dwight Braxton went after him following a fight

"Boxing is the last bastion of laissez-faire capitalism."

Mike Trainer, Sugar Ray Leonard's attorney

"You learn in life that there are always ups and downs. We must have enough sense to enjoy our ups and enough heart to get through our downs."

Mickey Walker, on what he learned from boxing

LIVINGSTONE BRAMBLE

"If he tries to change me, then he knows he ain't got no Bramble anymore."

Livingstone Bramble, on his manager, Lou Duva, trying to change the boxer's unorthodox style

"You know what I wish on Dave Wolf? Sometimes I wish he were Bramble's manager."

> Lou Duva, Bramble's manager,
> on Ray Mancini's manager, his
> longtime rival

"Every guy he fights has the home-world advantage."

> Mike Lupica, on Bramble

BUM

"You're still a bum, and so is Carnera."

> Bill Brown, New York Boxing
> Commissioner, to Max Baer, after
> Baer beat Primo Carnera (Brown
> had called Baer a bum before the
> Carnera fight)

"I'll moider da bum."

> Tony Galento, stating his fighting
> motto

"Fighting is the only racket where you're almost guaranteed to end up as a bum."
> *Rocky Graziano*

BUM OF THE MONTH

"I know what I'd do if I were you. I'd go out and make some money. I'd find some bums and start turning lights out left and right."
> *David Letterman, offering advice to*
> *Buster Douglas after Douglas*
> *defeated Mike Tyson*

"Thank heavens Joe Louis makes it quick and merciful."
> *Damon Runyon, on Louis's knocking*
> *out bum of the month Tami Mauriello*
> *in the first round*

"But I'm not fighting one bum a month. I'm fighting three or four."
> *Buck "Tombstone" Smith, responding*
> *to critics who claimed that his 110–2*
> *record was inflated because he fought*
> *a bum a month*

"To be a great champion, you must believe you are the best. If you're not, pretend you are."
Muhammad Ali

"More important than the President of the United States."
Muhammad Ali, on what the heavyweight championship means

"To tin-can around the country just for paydays and muffins is not my idea of living."
Muhammad Ali, on why someone would bother to fight if he were not fighting to be the champion

"The man who beat the man who beat the man who beat the man."
Riddick Bowe, on how he became heavyweight champion

"I guess I would buy new jeans."
Tex Cobb, asked what he would do if he were heavyweight champion

"I don't want nobody to call me champ until I beat Schmeling."

> Joe Louis, after beating James
> Braddock to become heavyweight
> champion

"I know that if I kept on fighting, some guy would come along and take the title away from me, but not this guy, never tonight."

> Joe Louis, asked if he ever thought
> about losing a fight

"What would be better than walking down any street in any city and knowing you're a champion?"

> Rocky Marciano

"Dempsey retired the word *champ* with him. Dempsey meant champ."

> Jim Murray, on Jack Dempsey

"It is something you don't give up without a hard struggle, even if you have to stagger out of there."

> Gene Tunney, on the heavyweight
> title

CHEAP

"Tommy Hearns squeezes a nickel so tight, the Indian sits on the buffalo."
Irving Rudd

CHICAGO, CHICAGO

"The first day I got there, I put my suitcase down, looked up at the Sears Tower, and said, 'Chicago, I'm going to conquer you.' When I looked down, my suitcase was gone."
James "Quick" Tillis

CHIN MUSIC

"I hit him as hard as I could, right on the chin. And down I went."
Art Aragon, after losing to Alvaro Guitierrez at the end of his career

"If they're that careful, they must be scared or something we don't know about. Perhaps he's got a potato for a chin."

> *Al Braverman, on Gerry Cooney's managers being very cautious with opponents they chose*

"You must aim like a marksman for the point of the chin. If you land, it is the end."

> *Georges Carpentier, heavyweight, explaining his theory on knockouts*

"Frank has no chin. Once he gets hit clean, he goes."

> *Mickey Duff, on Frank Bruno*

"A ham hock to the chin."

> *George Foreman, describing the punch he used to knock out Michael Moorer for the heavyweight title*

"You know them fighters with long necks and thin, long, pointy chins, they cost you more for smelling salts than they do for food."

> *Charlie Goldman, Rocky Marciano's trainer*

"Because he kept coming up to my chin all night."
> *Benny Leonard, asked how he lost to a fighter who only came up to his chin*

GEORGE CHUVALO

"I am the best heavyweight fighter in Canada, and I'll be the best until I'm dead seven years."
> *George Chuvalo, on being stripped of the title he held for 20 years as Canadian heavyweight champion*

"I just want to say I enjoyed the fight."
> *George Chuvalo, on being punched mercilessly by Ali but still managing not to get knocked out*

"He just keeps coming and coming. The only way you can stop him is with a stick of dynamite."
> *Bill Drover, Canada's No. 2 heavyweight behind Chuvalo*

CITY OF BROTHERLY LOVE

"I saw two winos fighting in a Philly alley once and one of them was throwing out double jabs."

> *Tex Cobb, on how everyone in*
> *Philadelphia knows how to box*

"It's not a town, it's a jungle. They don't have gyms. They have zoos. They don't have sparring sessions. They have wars."

> *Angelo Dundee, on Philadelphia*

THE CLASSICS

"I predict that this will be the greatest book ever and it will sell more than any other book in history."

> *Muhammad Ali, on* The Greatest

"When it is all finished and I write a book, if I do, the title will be *The Only Thing Square Was the Ring.*"

> *Bob Biron, fight manager*

"I would like to write about the boyhood of Cassius Clay, about his family, about his hopes and ambitions. That material would come in handy when it came time to write the full story of Cassius Clay, world champion."

Cassius Clay, predicting his future early in his career

"The Rock don't know too much about the boxing book, but it wasn't a book he hit me with. It was a whole library of bone crushers."

Joe Louis, on Rocky Marciano

"Uncle Will Gibson's career is book material, but I don't think that it will ever be written, because a recitation of his memoirs might tend to embarrass a number of his fellow citizens."

Westbrook Pegler, journalist, on promoter Billy Gibson

"Let's have prizefighters with harder wallops and less Shakespeare."

Will Rogers, on Gene Tunney's love of Shakespeare

"Don't invite Cassius Clay and Sonny Liston to the same party. It seems last time they almost had a fight."

Anonymous, on the lack of action in the first Clay–Liston bout

"In Miami I was Columbus, I was traveling into the unknown. I had to be cautious because I didn't know what to expect."

Cassius Clay, on being nervous before the fight

"I would make Liston think he was fighting 10 guys. I would have him so dizzy, he would think he was on a carousel."

Cassius Clay, before the fight

"I will kiss his feet in front of the whole world, tell him that he is the greatest, and take the first jet out of the good old U.S.A."

Cassius Clay, asked what he would do if Liston beat him

"Liston's case of homicide against Patterson."

Cassius Clay, before the fight,
describing Liston's defeat of Floyd
Patterson two minutes into the first
round

"Who would have thought when they came to the fight that they'd witness the launchin' of a human satellite."

Cassius Clay

"Clay needs a lesson in manners. Maybe I can help him by beating his brains out."

Sonny Liston, on the fight

"I'll get locked up for murder if I fight him. He can't lick a Popsicle."

Sonny Liston, on Clay

"He should be arrested for impersonating a fighter."

Sonny Liston, on Clay

"Two rounds—one and a half to ketch him, and a half a round to lick him."

> Sonny Liston, asked to predict the length of the fight

"Bill took his licking standing up. Liston took his sitting down."

> Willie Ratner, sportswriter, on promoter Bill McDonald, who took a bath on the fight

CLAY—LISTON II

"The crowd would not dream, when they laid down their money, that they would see a total eclipse of the Sonny."

> Cassius Clay, anticipating the rematch with Liston

"My big mouth overshadowed my ability."

> Cassius Clay, on not being appreciated for beating Liston twice

"When I beat him again, he will be finished as a title contender. He may want to stick around for paydays, but nobody will talk of him as a heavyweight contender."

Cassius Clay

"If I said I would knock out Sonny Liston in 1 minute and 49 seconds of the first round, that would hurt the gate."

Cassius Clay, before the fight, which he won in 1 minute and 52 seconds

"Yeah, a bad night."

Sonny Liston, asked if he had any predictions for Clay before the fight

CLEVELAND

"I spent a year there one Sunday."

Jake LaMotta

"I have more room for improvement than most heavyweights in this business."
Tex Cobb

"If I were any more serious, they'd make me a national disease."
Tex Cobb, on being accused of not taking things seriously

"Don't bother the man, he's busy."
Tex Cobb, after the referee warned Earnie Shavers to stop holding and hitting Cobb

"Randy might as well be fighting for a living. I mean, he'd be out fighting somewhere Friday night anyway."
Friend of Tex Cobb, on Cobb's facing Larry Holmes in a Friday-night fight

"He is boxing's Rogers these days. Will outside the ring, Fred within."

> *Richard Hoffer, reporter, on Cobb's being friendly outside the ring and a patsy inside the ring*

"Randy has a puss like a bruised biscuit. It looks like somebody painted eyes, lips, and nose holes on a wad of dough."

> *Blackie Sherrod, reporter, on Cobb*

COLLEGE YEARS

"I went two years and majored in probation."

> *Tex Cobb, on college life at Abilene Christian*

"My 11-year-old daughter, a straight-A student, would be very disappointed in me had I passed up the chance to go to Harvard."

> *George Foreman, on being honored by the* Harvard Lampoon

"You didn't make a dime out of it, but maybe I can get you a varsity letter."

> *Doc Kearns, on Mickey Walker's*
> *taking on 10 Notre Dame football*
> *players in a bar*

"Boxing is the only sport that didn't go to college."
> *Tony Zale*

COME FLY WITH ME

"This plane isn't going to crash. I'm on it."

> *Muhammad Ali, speaking to a*
> *nervous passenger during a turbulent*
> *flight*

"Superman don't need no plane."

> *A flight attendant, after she*
> *instructed Muhammad Ali to put on*
> *his seat belt and he said, "Superman*
> *don't need no seat belt"*

"I've never seen an old fighter come back without it being for money."

> George Benton, trainer

"I'd take on anybody—providing they could find a place for me to stay, because my family would put me out of the house."

> Joe Frazier, discussing a possible comeback

"Stepping-stones can be hard to break."

> Kevin Howard, on being called a stepping-stone for the comeback of Sugar Ray Leonard

"I'm waiting for someone to break the record so that I can start a comeback."

> Archie Moore, at age 80, on his record of fighting professionally to age 50

"We don't want a requiem for a heavyweight played on NBC."

> *Ferdie Pacheco, on why NBC*
> *wouldn't cover a fight featuring the*
> *comeback of 37-year-old Joe Frazier*

COMMUNICATIONS BREAKDOWN

"I knock him out in two rounds."

> *Primo Carnera, who spoke little*
> *English, when asked how he liked*
> *Los Angeles*

"No, we had some rapid communications, but it wasn't verbal."

> *Tex Cobb, asked if he talked to Larry*
> *Holmes during their 15-round fight*

"He's a nice guy. I like him. He's a good guy. But I wanted to kill him."

> *Rocky Graziano, after his second fight with Tony Zale*

"He only wants to fight cripples, old people, and guys who can't fight."

> *Marvin Hagler, on Tommy Hearns*

"Ali's ass is grass and I'm the lawn mower."

> *Larry Holmes, before fighting Ali*

"I fought maybe three, four hundred fights, and every one was a pleasure."

> *Sam Langford*

"Every time Joe Louis hit me, he said, 'Sorry.' Every time Jack Dempsey hit me, he said, 'How come you're not dead yet?'"

> *Jack Sharkey, comparing the fighting styles of Louis and Dempsey*

HENRY COOPER

"His potatoes kept getting cut eyes."
> *Reggie Gutteridge, British*
> *sportswriter, on boxer Henry Cooper,*
> *who retired to become a gardener*

"He is the nicest fellow ever to be about to be defeated for the world heavyweight title."
> *Hugh McIlvanney, British journalist,*
> *before Cooper fought Cassius Clay*

CORNER

"What's the use? I got to get right up again, ain't I?"
> *John L. Sullivan, explaining his*
> *refusal to sit between rounds in a*
> *76-round fight with Jake Kilrain*

"They were so small you had to share the corner with your opponent."
> *Chuck Wepner, on the small clubs in*
> *which he fought*

CORNERMEN

"All I know is when the bell rings, I walk up the steps and they walk down the steps."

> *Buster Mathis, on his cornermen*

"Amateur cornermen speak quietly and more grammatically correct."

> *Ferdie Pacheco, on the difference between amateur and professional cornermen*

HOWARD COSELL

"Howard Cosell would rather shave a wild lion with a dull razor than fight me."

> *Muhammad Ali, responding to rumors that Cosell wanted to fight him*

"Howard Cosell is nobody's fool . . . he's everybody's fool."

> *Muhammad Ali*

"Sometimes Howard makes me wish I was a dog and he was a fireplug."

Muhammad Ali

"I know. I got a thank-you letter from his wife."

Tex Cobb, when told Cosell had complained that he would miss Thanksgiving dinner because he had to cover a Holmes–Cobb fight

"I'd go 15 more rounds with Holmes if I thought it would get Cosell off football broadcasts."

Tex Cobb, after Cosell said, following a Holmes–Cobb fight, that he would stop announcing boxing

"He doesn't know much about sports. He talks sports like a lawyer—like he's addressing a jury."

Rocky Graziano, on Cosell

"If Cosell's gonna call it, I won't fight Cooney again."

Larry Holmes, after Cosell said he would announce a Larry Holmes–Gerry Cooney rematch

"Howard, there's one fewer than you think there is."

> *Harry Markson, promoter, responding to Cosell's claim that there are few good sports announcers*

"Not while I'm alive."

> *Irving Rudd, publicist, after Cosell's statement that he was his own worst enemy*

"[He] demonstrated time and again that he knows very little about the game but is not afraid to describe it."

> *Burt Sugar, on Cosell*

CRUISERWEIGHTS

"It's just one step. The next step, I need to go get a title that people really know."

> *Tommy Hearns, on winning the WBU Cruiserweight Championship*

CUBA

"I'm going to whip you, then Castro."
>   *Riddick Bowe, on fighting Jorge Luis*
>   *Gonzales of Cuba*

"What is 8 million dollars against 8 million Cubans who love me?"
>   *Teofilo Stevenson, on not making*
>   *money as a great heavyweight from*
>   *Cuba*

CUT MAN

"He'll have a lot of fun. George will keep him in stitches."
>   *Ferdie Pacheco, on Angelo Dundee's*
>   *agreeing to be George Foreman's cut*
>   *man*

DANCING MACHINE

"When I'm dancin' and runnin'—I'm looking pretty and winnin', but ain't hurtin'."
Muhammad Ali

"We've got to put our tap shoes on. I'm an entertainer."
Pernell Whitaker, on beating Buddy McGirt

DEATH AND TAXES

"I'd like them to check this organization known as the IRS, because they recognize me as champion."
Muhammad Ali, on Ernie Terrell's being recognized by the WBA as champion while Ali was being investigated by the IRS

"They're like relatives. They're always knocking on the door. I'm the one in there taking all the punches. I get the hell beat out of me and they're taking all my money."

Bob Foster, on the IRS

"They buried me, cremated me, put me back in the grave."

Joe Frazier, on his performance in two bouts after spending a week in the hospital following the first Ali fight

"Everybody wants to go to heaven, but nobody wants to die."

Joe Louis

"When I was boxing, I made $5 million and wound up broke, owing the government a million. If I was boxing today, I'd make $10 million and wind up broke owing the government 2 million."

Joe Louis

"Start counting—he will get up at nine."

Wilson Mizner, reporter, on the death of boxer Stanley Ketchel

"Nah, I'm not dead. I ain't even been out of the house."

> *Willie Pep, on reports he had died*

"I'd rather get the money and enjoy it now. If I die right now, someone will say, 'So what do we do with all this stuff?' "

> *Chuck Wepner, on selling his boxing memorabilia*

JACK DEMPSEY

"A Dempsey fight was magic. The minute he walked into the ring you could see the smoke rising from the canvas."

> *Ray Arcel*

"He could hit you once on top of the head and finish you."

> *Ray Arcel*

"He was shaking off my punches as if I was patting him with my open hand."

> *Georges Carpentier*

"Push me back in there, somebody."

Jack Dempsey, after being knocked out of the ring by Luis Firpo

"Rickard played the cards, but the ace of spades was, as it always is, the highest card on the deck. Dempsey was it."

Paul Gallico, referring to Dempsey and promoter Tex Rickard

" 'There goes Jack Dempsey,' they say wherever he goes, and he's still Jack Dempsey."

Frank Graham, on how the legend lives on despite Dempsey's longtime retirement

"He was a killer—a superhuman wildman. . . . His complete intent was an opponent's destruction."

Grantland Rice

DEMPSEY—TUNNEY I

"Lead me out there. I want to shake his hand."

Jack Dempsey, after Tunney beat him easily in their first fight

"I forgot to duck."

> *Jack Dempsey, after the fight,*
> *explaining to his wife what happened*

"Let me say that Tunney might have defeated me at any time in our career. On that rainy night in Philadelphia, he needed no help."

> *Jack Dempsey*

"The public took the beaten villain to its heart, loved him again, and dubbed him hero."

> *Paul Gallico, on Dempsey's*
> *gracefully losing to Tunney*

"If a guy had you down in an alley, beating the hell out of you, who would you holler for, Dempsey or Tunney?"

> *Jim Hussey, promoter, on why he bet*
> *and lost a lot of money on Dempsey*

"The greatest swinging exhibition I have ever witnessed."

> *Jimmy Walker, mayor of New York*
> *City*

DEMPSEY—TUNNEY II
(THE LONG COUNT)

"People remember the long count more than
anything in my entire career. They never have
stopped sympathizing with me. It has been money
in the bank. And I love money."
Jack Dempsey

DIRTY POOL

"I coulda busted Joe Louis up real good if my
manager woulda let me get out there and hit him
all over. You know what I mean . . . Butt him and
kick him around. It's a fight, isn't it?"
Tony Galento

"You win some, you throw some."
Jake LaMotta

"Your head is your best hand—there's no glove
on it."
A. J. Liebling

"Boxing is a great sport and a dirty business."
Ken Norton

"Once some gamblers made me a very attractive offer to take a dive in the second round, but I turned them down—I couldn't go the distance."
Maxie Rosenbloom

"Rocky Graziano didn't box, he threw cobblestones. If permitted, he would cheerfully have used a knife or blade or grenade."
Red Smith

"My three best punches were the choke hold, the rabbit punch, and the head butt."
Chuck Wepner

"If Johnson threw the fight, I wish he'd thrown it sooner. It was hotter than hell down there."
Jess Willard, on Jack Johnson's claiming he threw a fight with Willard by being knocked out in the 26th round

"I'd give 'em the head, choke 'em . . . but never in my life use my thumb, because I wanted no one to use it on me. . . . I used to bang 'em pretty good. You're fighting, you're not playing the piano, you know."

Fritzie Zivic

"Me a dirty fighter? Nah. Every time I hit a guy low, I'd say, 'Pardon me.'"

Fritzie Zivic

DOCTOR IN THE HOUSE

"No, dummy, a people doctor."

Max Baer, after calling for a doctor in a hotel and being asked by the operator if he wanted a hotel doctor

"When the doctor slapped me on my rear, and I hit him with a left hook."

Duane Bobick, asked when he started boxing

"**W**ho are those doctors? Where did they come from? They could be veterinarians, for all we know."

> *Lou Duva, Livingstone Bramble's trainer, claiming that cuts to Ray Mancini should have ended the fight sooner*

"**H**ow would I know? I'm a politician, not a doctor."

> *Sonny McDonough, Boston politician, asked what was wrong with Clay after the second fight with Liston was canceled*

"**I** absolutely agree. The British Medical Association should not box—but leave it to the professional fighters."

> *Sylvester Stallone, after the British Medical Association recommended the banning of boxing*

BUSTER DOUGLAS

"The No. 1 contender in the latest ring rankings from *Mad* magazine."

> *Mike Downey*, Los Angeles Times,
> *on making Buster Douglas the No. 1*
> *contender before the Tyson fight*

DREAM ON

"If anyone even dreams he can beat me, he had better wake up and apologize."

> *Muhammad Ali*

"Yes, I've had dreams about a lot of my fights. In my dreams, I'm undefeated."

> *Chuck Wepner, on dreaming about*
> *beating Ali*

DRIVE MY CAR

"In that case, you get in the backseat and I'll do the driving."

> *Maxie Rosenbloom, to his limo driver, whom he owed $150*

MICKEY DUFF

"Where there's Hope, there's Duff."

> *Mike Marley, on Mickey Duff, the ubiquitous English trainer of Maurice Hope*

ANGELO DUNDEE

"In that one minute, Angelo is Godzilla and Superman rolled into one."

> *Ferdie Pacheco, on Dundee's activity between rounds*

"The only time Duran is serious is when he's sleeping or when he's fighting."
Freddie Brown

"If Duran isn't going to fight anymore, we'd love to sign him. He's just our kind of guy—a quitter."
Harold Guiver, vice president of the hapless New Orleans Saints, inquiring about Duran after his "No Mas" fight

"Duran walks around like snow is supposed to melt under him. He's a living legend, and I made him look like an amateur."
Sugar Ray Leonard, after his second fight with Duran

"That would send any sensible grown man home to change the locks and upgrade the security system."
Leigh Montville, on Duran's legendary stare

"When Duran is 65 years old, he'll be fighting for nickels in the street."

> *Alvaro Riet, Duran's interpreter, on Duran's love for boxing*

"They're making a romantic figure out of a guy [who], if they ran into him in a bar, they'd throw up."

> *Mike Trainer, Sugar Ray Leonard's attorney*

EGO

"When you're as great as I am, it's hard to be humble."

> *Muhammad Ali*

"This is the story about a man with iron fists and a beautiful tan. He talks a lot indeed about a powerful punch and blinding speed."

> *Muhammad Ali, describing himself in a book written about him*

"The most spectacular wonder human eyes have ever witnessed."

Muhammad Ali, on himself

"When I'm gone, boxing be nothing again."

Muhammad Ali

"Braggin' is when a person says something and can't do it. I do what I say."

Muhammad Ali

"If there's fighting after I'm gone, it'll just be a dull old thing. No more poems, no predictions, no more hollering."

Muhammad Ali

"A stubborn, cocky, supercilious know-it-all."

Art Aragon, self-description

"I'm a fair boxer, a fair puncher, but I put it together and it works."

Duane Bobick

"I am told that I should develop some modesty. Why? What good can modesty do me? How much can I sell modesty for? How is it sold? By the quart or by the pound?"

Cassius Clay, in his pre-Ali years

"My cause is me."

Joe Frazier, asked why he didn't have any causes, as Muhammad Ali did

"My biggest difficulty is assuaging egos. It's like getting every great actor in the world in the same movie."

Don King, on having several top-rank boxers in the same stable

"When I gaze into the mirror, I never cease to amaze myself. And I say this humbly."

Don King

"I knew I had him when I signed for the fight."

Joe Louis, asked when he knew he was going to beat James Braddock

"No, I ain't never thought he could beat me."

> *Sugar Ray Robinson, asked if he ever*
> *thought he could lose a fight before*
> *the fight had started*

"Hector Camacho's great dream is to someday die in his own arms."

> *Irving Rudd*

"I can lick any man in the house."

> *John L. Sullivan, whenever he*
> *entered a bar*

"I've got Muhammad Ali's wit, face, and grace. I've got Sugar Ray's hands. And I've got Jack Johnson's pace."

> *Elijah Tillery*

ENTOURAGE

"It varies depending on the city. It's always between 29 and 100."

> *Angelo Dundee, on the size of Ali's*
> *entourage*

"Leon says, 'I'm going to run out in front of a tractor-trailer and watch it fall apart when it hits me.' And the tap dancers say, 'You right, champ.'"

> *Butch Lewis, on the entourage Leon*
> *Spinks picked up after beating Ali*

"For aging boxers, first your legs go, then your reflexes go, then your friends go."

> *Willie Pep*

"They may get over the fence, they might con my dogs, but they won't get past Laverne. She's in charge of entourages."

> *Earnie Shavers, on how his wife*
> *would prevent him from ever having*
> *an entourage*

"I used to say to him, 'Tami, it ain't the punches in the ring makes a fighter punchy. It's the taps on the back from his friends.'"

> *Al Silvani, trainer of Tami Mauriello*

"There was something in that charcoal, the other side had put some bad stuff in it, and it weakened me."

> *Art Aragon, claiming he lost a fight in 1949 because there was bad charcoal heating his dressing room*

"A good promoter has always got to have a good excuse. . . . It doesn't matter how good the excuse is as long as you've got one."

> *Pete Ashlock, boxing promoter*

"He hurt himself reaching for an excuse."

> *Stan Hochman, sportswriter, on Gerry Cooney's claims he injured his shoulder before facing Larry Holmes*

"Boxers don't refer to them as excuses but as explanations."

> *Jim Jacobs*

EXPERIENCE

"I'd like to fight him again after I learn to box."
Ray Mercer, after being upset by
Larry Holmes

"Experience is overrated in the fight game. Usually by old men who nod wisely and at times speak stupidly."
Archie Moore

FAMILY MATTERS

"Jim can use the title. He has five kids. . . . I don't know how many I have."
Max Baer, after losing the
heavyweight title to Jim Braddock

"Sorry, I can't fight Louis for you. I'll be busy this summer. I can't disappoint my relatives in Czechoslovakia. I promised to visit them."
Joe Baksi, English boxer, upon being
asked to fight Joe Louis

"Go out and call her right up, then come back and enjoy the fight."

Harry Balogh, famed boxing announcer, paging someone in the crowd whose mother had just had a stroke

"I like to think I'm a little henpecked myself."

Drew "Bundini" Brown, promoter, explaining why he was not upset that Tex Cobb pulled out of a fight to be with his wife, who was expecting a baby

"I would rather he was a dustman [trash collector] or a road sweeper than a professional boxer."

Joe Bugner, on his hope that his son not choose to follow in his footsteps

"All my father and I had in common was our name."

Marcel Cerdan Jr., on a lousy career as a boxer

"We were poor when the kids were named. This way they could share the shirts with *DD* initials on them."

> *Lou Duva, on naming his kids Dan, Denise, Donna, Dino, and Deanne*

"My whole family likes to play basketball. George II plays for his high school team. George III and George IV and George V are going to be good players. One day we're going to have a team and call it Georgetown."

> *George Foreman*

"As in red light. You know, no more kids."

> *George Foreman, asked why his ninth child is named Red*

"If I said, 'Fall down,' he's gonna fall down. I'm still his father."

> *Joe Frazier, asked what would happen if he fought his son Marvis*

"If I'd known how much fun it was, I'd have missed the middle steps of having kids."

> *Gene Fullmer, on grandchildren*

"I wouldn't want a dog to go through what I went through. I wouldn't even want my mother-in-law to go through it."

> *Larry Holmes, on bad publicity he receives*

"My father came in and started yelling at me. 'Viper, tramp, fighting for what?' I took out the five dollars I earned and handed it to him. He looked at it, smiled, and put his arms around me. 'That's all right, Benny, when are you going to fight again?'"

> *Benny Leonard, on getting his parents' approval in the fight game*

"Relatives are bad for fighters. They should be outside the ring."

> *Benny Leonard, on having his brother as his trainer*

"My love for her is greater than my love for the game that has made me independently wealthy, and to whom I owe all I now possess. But it must be so."

> *Benny Leonard, who retired at his mother's request*

"It's a one-two combination they're working on Tyson. His wife and his mother-in-law. That's a tough combination to beat."

Jackie Mason, on Mike Tyson's marriage to Robin Givens

"Not only will I fight him, but I'll fight his brother, Leon. I want to beat the whole family. If there're any other brothers, I'll beat them too."

James Scott, on fighting Michael Spinks

"You're messing with my money. I got to feed my babies."

Earnie Shavers, who was expecting a big payday for fighting Larry Holmes and watched Holmes almost lose to Mike Weaver

FAN CLUBS

"He is the soft-fleshed, hard-faced person who keeps his own pelt safe from bruises, but whose eyes glisten and whose hackles lift at the prospect of seeing somebody else whipped to a soufflé."

Irving Cobb, on the typical fight fan

"I thank the crowd for all that. I just wish they'd be the ones doing the voting."

> *Tex Cobb, on the big fan support he received when he fought Larry Holmes*

"If we fought, all the people on Geritol would come out of the woodwork. They'd have to make extra batteries so the old folks could tune in the fight on the radio."

> *George Foreman, on fighting Mike Tyson*

"You can beat him all you want, but he's the guy the fans go for, he's a living doll."

> *Frankie Genaro, on the popularity of flyweight Pancho Villa*

"Unless you've been in the ring when the noise is for you, there's no way you'll ever know what it's like."

> *Sugar Ray Robinson*

FARMING

"Farmers can't live off last year's crops."

> *Don King, asked whether Mike Tyson*
> *would fight after leaving prison*

"Like the farmer who has returned his profits to the soil—boxing is my soul."

> *Don King, on wanting to give back to*
> *boxing*

FIGHT SITES

"This place is so tough the canaries sing bass."

> *Bugs Baer, sportswriter, on Shelby,*
> *Montana, where Jack Dempsey*
> *fought Tom Gibbons*

"It's the only place where everybody is careful to lock up their bicycles but nobody bothers to lock their door."

> *Dick Gregory, on Riddick Bowe's*
> *training camp in a quiet, health-*
> *conscious town in Oregon*

"I can remember when a world heavyweight championship prizefight would be held in a place like Kingston, Jamaica, only if one or both of the principals was wanted by the police, his draft board, his creditors, or his ex-wives."

Jim Murray, on the first Frazier–Foreman fight, held in Kingston, Jamaica

FOOD FACTS

"I did that on hash. Get me a couple of steaks and there's no telling what I'll do."

James Braddock, after defeating John "Corn" Griffin in seven rounds

"If he doesn't act right, I'll bite his goddamn ears off."

Livingstone Bramble, a vegetarian, before a bout with Ray Mancini

"Foreman said you couldn't expect him to go 18 minutes without eating."

> *Lou Duva, on the contract between George Foreman and Evander Holyfield stipulating a 15-minute break after Round 6*

"He's a tough cookie, but I'm the big piece of cake."

> *George Foreman, on Mike Tyson*

"I'm going to eat hamburgers and cheeseburgers. I'm going to belly-bump him all over the ring."

> *George Foreman, explaining his fighting strategy against Evander Holyfield*

"He's got a nutritionist and I've got room service."

> *George Foreman, on differences between his and Evander Holyfield's training styles*

"I told them sandwiches."

> *George Foreman, asked before an appearance on* Home Improvement *what he intended to build*

"My DNA is cheeseburgers."
George Foreman

"You're going to feed me at this thing, aren't you?"
George Foreman, after being invited
to speak at a dinner

"Today the biggest decisions I make aren't related to the heavyweight title. They are whether I visit McDonald's, Burger King, Wendy's, or Jack in the Box."
George Foreman

"I am not a glutton. I am an explorer of food."
Archie Moore

"Bakeries have destroyed more boxers than wine, women, and song."
Jim Murray

"Pizza, potato chips, candy bars, Popsicles, hamburgers, peanuts."
Greg Page, asked how he gained
weight between fights

"A rose by any other name will always eat."

Charley Rose, promoter with a big appetite

"I've been kidded about my appetite all my life, but I'm thankful it never let me down. It's as good now as it was 50 years ago."

Charley Rose

"I'm like a bottle of milk with gloves."

Jim Watt, on his pale complexion

FOOTBALL

"When Ali put down his gloves and picked up his fork, I put down my fork and picked up my gloves."

Ernie Holmes, Pittsburgh Steeler, on his boxing career

"They say that boxing is brutal and violent. But you have to look at the concept of football. They don't try to get to the quarterback to shake his hand."

Sugar Ray Leonard

"It's called football. These kids don't need a degree from MIT to understand a signing bonus."

Burt Sugar, on why there are no great heavyweights

FORE

"I'm the best. I just haven't played yet."

Muhammad Ali, on golf

"Billy Casper has won titles at more weight levels than Sugar Ray Leonard."

John Brodie, on the fluctuating weight of the golf star

GEORGE FOREMAN

"George has three acts. Three cons. When he was young, George had the bully con. When he came back, he had the religious con. Now he's got the show-biz con."

Teddy Atlas

"Right now Moorer's kind of like the guy who gave up home run number 715 to Hank Aaron. You know, infamous forever."

> *Teddy Atlas, Michael Moorer's*
> *trainer, after Moorer was knocked out*
> *by Foreman*

"George is a big truck, but if he runs over you, he'll kill you."

> *Larry Holmes*

"I know a way to beat George Foreman, but it involves shelling him for three days and then sending in the infantry."

> *Hugh McIlvanney, British*
> *sportswriter, on stopping Foreman*
> *early in the boxer's career*

"I could get out [of jail] on Tuesday and beat George on Wednesday."

> *Mike Tyson*

"TWO-TON"
TONY GALENTO

"You shoulda fought with three gloves . . . one on each hand, the other on your head."

> *Danny Rubino, on the legendary dirty fighting techniques of Tony Galento*

GOD BLESS THE U.S.A.

"I consider my opponents to be from other countries like Vietnam. Evander Holyfield—I consider him to be a big country like Iraq. And the U.S. has to win."

> *Riddick Bowe*

"I've made the national anthem a six-point underdog."

> *Jimmy the Greek, on Joe Frazier's singing the national anthem before a fight*

"How can we blame people for wanting to come to America? It's like holding a steak out to a wolf and telling him he can't have it."

> Don King, on Proposition 187 in
> California, which sought to bar
> immigration to California from
> Mexico

"The old pitcher went to the well once too often, but I'm glad the championship remains in America."

> John L. Sullivan, on losing the
> heavyweight championship by being
> knocked out by James Corbett in the
> 21st round

GOTTA HAVE HEART

"If you're hurt go to grass, and if you're a man stand up and fight."

> Jack "Nonpareil" Dempsey,
> challenging Johnny Regan during
> their 45-round fight on sand

"I got too much heart and stamina to be his valentine over the 15-round route."

> *Jake LaMotta, on fighting Sugar Ray*
> *Robinson for the sixth time on*
> *Valentine's Day, 1951*

"I have the heart of a racehorse trapped inside the body of a jackass."

> *Tracy Steele, who lost six of nine*
> *pro fights*

THE GREATEST

"That he took a few cups of love and one teaspoon of patience. One tablespoon of generosity. One pint of kindness. One quart of laughter. Mixed it up and stirred it well. And then he spread it over the span of a lifetime and served it to each and every deserving person he met."

> *Muhammad Ali, on how he would*
> *like to be remembered*

"One can only hope that, to put it ineptly, someone will succeed in knocking some sense into Clay's head before he is done damaging the spirit of the country."

> *William Buckley, political commentator, on Cassius Clay's refusal to be drafted*

"Muhammad Ali is Muhammad Ali, and compared to him all other men are earthlings."

> *Angelo Dundee*

"I want him now. I didn't want him in the '70s, but I want him now."

> *George Foreman, on wanting to fight Ali 20 years after their fight in Zaire*

"He floats like an anchor, stings like a moth."

> *Ray Gandolf, on Ali at age 39*

"Ali's mind is making a date his body can't keep."

> *Larry Holmes, on Ali's comeback against him*

"He has an unlisted phone number, but everybody knows it."

> *Gene Kilroy, Ali aide, on the*
> *accessibility of The Greatest*

"Only if he ties a 56-pound weight to each leg."

> *Brian London, asked if he wanted a*
> *rematch against Ali after Ali beat*
> *London convincingly*

"He's a guy with a million dollars' worth of confidence and a dime's worth of courage. I could have whipped him."

> *Joe Louis*

"When I was fighting, I went on a Bum of the Month tour. I didn't say Clay is a bum. I say he would have been on the tour."

> *Joe Louis*

"He is America's Greatest Ego."

> *Norman Mailer*

"He won't be satisfied 'til Michelangelo paints him and hangs him on the Vatican ceiling."

> *Jim Murray*

"It worked for Muhammad Ali—it won't work with anyone else. If you want to be a comedian, go into show business."

> Carlos Ortiz, on fighters who try to intimidate each other before the fight

"Anything he wanted to do, anytime he wanted to do it."

> Ferdie Pacheco, on how Ali would have fared against Tyson

"MARVELOUS" MARVIN HAGLER

"There are currently two middleweight divisions: Hagler and the rest."

> Hugh McIlvanney, British sportswriter, on the greatness of Marvin Hagler

"No, I'm gonna starve myself."

> Davey Moore, junior middleweight, asked if he would gain weight to fight Hagler

"If he had a part in a movie, he'd be the guy guarding the gang hideout—'You want I should punch his head off, boss?'"

Jim Murray, on Hagler

HAIR CARE

"I see my hair, a burning bush basted in righteous justice."

Don King

"The truth is that my hair is an aura from God. . . . He made every streak a citadel."

Don King

HALL OF FAME

"I guess I outlived all my critics."

Jack Sharkey, on his election to the Boxing Hall of Fame

HATS OFF

"I just can't keep a white hat clean. I just like a black hat."

> *Tex Cobb, on why he likes portraying a villain by wearing a black hat*

HEAD GAMES

"When you lose your head, you lose the best part of your body."

> *Ray Arcel*

"I'm a headhunter. Keep punching at a man's head and it mixes his mind."

> *Cassius Clay*

"I learned a lot about stamina, a lot about jabbing. You may have noticed, though, I didn't learn a lot about moving my head."

> *Tex Cobb, on getting hit in the head a great deal during a 15-round fight against Larry Holmes*

"People always ask if success is going to change me,
and I tell them I sure hope so."

Tex Cobb

TOMMY "HIT MAN" HEARNS

"He's going to run to his corner and ask Emanuel
Stewart, 'What do I do now?' If Emanuel is smart,
he'll go and tell him to pray."

> *Marvin Hagler, on how Tommy
> Hearns, whose trainer was Emanuel
> Stewart, would react to fighting
> Hagler*

HEAT IS ON

"I lasted longer than Goldstein, and nobody was
hitting him."

> *Sugar Ray Robinson, on losing to
> Joey Maxim in 100-degree heat that
> caused referee Rudy Goldstein to
> faint*

HEAVEN HELP US

"Somebody up there likes me."
Rocky Graziano

HEAVYWEIGHT DIVISION

"Small guys can't raise any hell."
*Muhammad Ali, on why Americans
are fascinated by heavyweights*

"A heavyweight is always one punch away from redemption."
Tommy Morrison

"The quality of heavyweight fighters, like the length of skirts and the price of cabbage, is given to periodic fluctuations."
William Nack, sportswriter

"It has something to do with being American. Americans are always obsessed with big things—cars, houses, breasts, fighters."

> *Bert Sugar, on Americans' love of heavyweights*

HECKLERS

"I got this way from 289 fights. What's your excuse?"

> *Maxie Rosenbloom, interrupted by a heckler during his nightclub routine*

HIGHWAY ROBBERY

"I let him rob my house while I was out to lunch."

> *Muhammad Ali, after losing the heavyweight title to Leon Spinks*

"We wuz robbed."

> *Joe Jacobs, Max Schmeling's trainer, after Schmeling lost a controversial decision to Jack Sharkey*

HOCKEY

"I went to a fight the other night and a hockey game broke out."

Rodney Dangerfield

LARRY HOLMES

"He's 34. He's 40–0 and he's due to have a bad night. He can't keep up this crap forever."

Tex Cobb, on his chances of beating Larry Holmes

"I'd like to fight him every day of the week, because eventually he'd get tired."

Tex Cobb

"I wondered the same thing myself."

Tex Cobb, asked how he managed to stay up for 15 rounds while Holmes was pounding him

"What the hell is this guy going to do to me? Hit me? You think I got all this scar tissue running into parked cars?"

> *Tex Cobb, asked if he felt intimidated by Larry Holmes*

"I don't think his hands could take the abuse."

> *Tex Cobb, on fighting Holmes again*

"If we gotta wait for you to beat Larry Holmes, we ain't never gonna fight, so we better think of some other way."

> *Tex Cobb, to Renaldo Snipes, who said he would fight Cobb after beating Holmes*

"Well, it wasn't how to get out of the way."

> *Tex Cobb, asked if he had learned anything from fighting Holmes*

HOMETOWN

"Population 327 . . . and that's counting the cows."

> *Angelo Dundee, on Tulsa, Oklahoma, home of James "Quick" Tillis*

"Here the Joneses try to keep up with the Holmeses."

> *Larry Holmes, on his hometown of Easton, Pennsylvania*

"Every town has its Top 10 toughest guys. I wanted to be in the Top 10 in Tuscaloosa."

> *Edgar "Mad Dog" Ross, junior welterweight*

"Listen to those police sirens—man, we've got a police escort and we ain't even in trouble."

> *Michael Spinks, to his brother Leon, during a parade in St. Louis honoring them for winning gold medals in the Olympics*

"I have no intention of defending the title outside of my home city."

> *Jim Watt, asked if he would do everything he could to retain his lightweight title*

"Nah, I'm from Missouri. You gotta show me."

> *Chuck Wepner, asked if he was afraid of facing Sonny Liston*

"This face is worth billions."

>   *Muhammad Ali, on why he would be*
>   *a very successful actor*

"I got to be the hero. Like Charlton Heston, he's got a serious image. Moses. In *Airport*, he was the captain, a real man. Always distinguished. Always high-class. Nothing cheap or low-down."

>   *Muhammad Ali, on his acting*
>   *aspirations*

"I couldn't believe it. I got the role without your testing me."

>   *Muhammad Ali, on playing himself*
>   *in the movie version of* The Greatest

"I took a nobody and created a monster. I made Norton so famous, he even got on *The Dating Game*."

>   *Muhammad Ali, on losing to Ken*
>   *Norton*

"I'll be greater than all the stars in Hollywood. They'll make cartoons about me. I'll be inhuman."

Muhammad Ali, on his attempts to win a fourth title

"They could make 10 films from my life."

Muhammad Ali, on his movie The Greatest

"It will be the best-selling movie ever. I can outdraw Charlton Heston, Clint Eastwood, Marlon Brando, and John Wayne rolled into one."

Muhammad Ali, on The Greatest

"I can act well enough for them to pay me $31 million since I have been in boxing. So I act pretty good."

Muhammad Ali, asked if he could act for his role in The Greatest

"They're always wanting to put lipstick and rouge on me."

Billy Conn, asked why he did not appear in a movie about his life

"I almost ruined the American theater."

> *Jack Dempsey, on acting in a play on*
> *Broadway*

"He couldn't knock your hat off."

> *Jack Dempsey, on sparring with*
> *Rudolph Valentino*

"Well, laddie, that's show business."

> *Mickey Duff, promoter of a fighter*
> *who lost decisively to Matthew Saad*
> *Muhammad*

"If he's so damn good as an actor, why did he ever become a fighter?"

> *Bob Fitzsimmons, on James Corbett's*
> *avoiding having to fight him, using*
> *his acting career as an excuse*

"There's too much singing."

> *Sonny Liston, asked why he walked*
> *out of the musical* The Flower Drum
> Song

"A boxing match is like a cowboy movie. There's got to be good guys and there's got to be bad guys, so I'm a bad guy."

Sonny Liston

"It was like a song from a movie I just saw. It went, 'Tommy, can you hear me.'"

> *Rock Newman, Riddick Bowe's*
> *manager, after witnessing a bad*
> *Holyfield–Alex Stewart fight that*
> *made him think Bowe should face*
> *Tommy Morrison instead of Holyfield*

"Susan George seduces me, but after you get seduced 12 hours a day, two days straight, it's kinda hard to like it."

> *Ken Norton, on his role in* Mandingo

"I did a lot of work in front of cameras as a fighter, but we had no script."

> *Sugar Ray Robinson, comparing*
> *acting to boxing*

"Boxing is a great exercise—as long as you can yell 'cut' whenever you want to."

Sylvester Stallone

"He was trying to knock my block off. I don't mind waltzing a little bit, but you gotta show who the boss is."

> Tony Zale, on portraying himself in fight scenes for the movie Somebody Up There Likes Me *(Rocky Graziano's story) and things getting feisty in the ring with Paul Newman, who was portraying Graziano*

I COULDA BEEN
A CONTENDER

"I was always right on the edge of the top echelon. The edge seemed to be my destiny."

> Wilf Greaves, middleweight contender

"My punches hurt me more than they did Braddock."

> *Max Baer, who injured his hand*
> *while losing the heavyweight title to*
> *James Braddock*

"For $2 million, I'd have cut off my pinkie finger."
> *Marvin Hagler, on Thomas Hearns's*
> *putting off a fight with him,*
> *complaining of an injured finger*

"It seems like a thousand people a day ask me about it. I want to get a card printed up that I can hand out that says, 'The eye is OK.'"
> *Sugar Ray Leonard*

"A man who fights as often as I do has got a lot of things to watch. Every time I put my title on the line, I've got a million dollars ridin'. A broken hand or cut eye can cost me plenty."
> *Joe Louis*

"He introduced a mental capacity in a sport where illiteracy was an outstanding characteristic."

James Dawson, on Jim Corbett

"To be a fighter, you can't be a smart guy. To get in the ring with anybody to fight, you got to be a little wacky."

Rocky Graziano

"Dempsey checks his brains in the dressing room."

Harry Greb, on Jack Dempsey

"Clay insult me? I'm too ignorant."

Brian London, asked if he was offended by the insults being leveled at him by Cassius Clay

"The best fighter in the world from the neck down."

William Muldoon, trainer of John L. Sullivan, on the stupidity of Jack Sharkey

"I know a lot of people think I'm dumb. Well, at least I ain't no educated fool."
Leon Spinks

"You cannot be only smart in boxing and stupid in other things. It's impossible for you to be a stupid guy and be a smart fighter."
Jose Torres

"Perhaps in his mind he's very serious, but everyone knows that Larry Holmes sometimes speaks before his brain is in motion."
Mike Tyson, responding to claims that Holmes would beat him

JACK JOHNSON

"I could never have whipped Jack Johnson at my best."
James Jeffries

"Jack Johnson was the greatest. And I tell you that honestly, because I hated Johnson."
Tom Sharkey

"Jack Johnson could've handled Joe Louis and Billy Conn simultaneously."

Jess Willard

ED "TOO TALL" JONES

"Ed evidently learned how to keep his eyes open in boxing. He's staying awake in meetings a lot better since he's come back."

Larry Cole, Cowboys teammate of Jones, on what Too Tall learned in his short-lived boxing career

"He looks pretty bad as a boxer, as far as I'm concerned. I think he should go back to football."

Joe Frazier

"I think the press expects too much of me. I think they expect me to fight the way I played football."

Ed "Too Tall" Jones

"At 6'9" and 253 pounds, he cannot box, he cannot punch, and his chin gives off a musical tinkle when it's tapped."

Red Smith

JUDGES

"The two judges who had the fight a point apart should be led to a vision center by a seeing-eye dog."

> Peter Finney, sportswriter, after
> Wilfred Benitez soundly defeated
> Roberto Duran

"This is K [his right hand] and this is O [his left hand]. These are my judges."

> Marvin Hagler, on why he doesn't
> care about judges in fights

DOC KEARNS

"Dad was 80 but he had the mind of a man of 20 and the body of a man 125."

> Jack Kearns Jr., on his father, the
> legendary fight manager

"Give Doc a hundred pounds of steel wool and he'll knit you a stove."

> *Archie Moore, on the amazing*
> *salesmanship of Kearns*

"I got robbed by the king of robbers. As long as I got robbed, I'm glad I got robbed by the best man in the country at robbing."

> *Jess Willard, on Doc Kearns's*
> *admitting he put plaster of paris in*
> *Jack Dempsey's gloves when Dempsey*
> *fought Willard*

DON KING

"He has scammed everybody he has ever been around. . . . If you got a quarter, he wants the first 26 cents."

> *Tex Cobb, on Don King*

"I love acting. It's easy for me. All you do is look in the camera, smile, and lie with charm. I learn how to do that watching Don King promote fights."

> *Tex Cobb*

"I decided I don't need this guy in my life no more. Let Tyson have it, all that cackling and lip-smacking."

George Foreman, on dumping King

"One day Don King will asphyxiate by the force of his own exhaust."

Carmen Graciano

"For 12 years, my lips were surgically attached to his ass."

Larry Holmes, on his relationship with Don King

"It's like someone saying your wife is committing adultery. You don't believe it until you see her slipping out of the motel with someone else."

Butch Lewis, on Greg Page's leaving Lewis for Don King

"Every time they count out Don King, he gets up. He's like a boxer. He grabs the ropes, pulls himself back up, and pulls out a victory."

Butch Lewis

"If they hadn't stopped it, Patterson would have won because Johansson was exhausted."

> *Anonymous, after Ingemar Johansson knocked down Floyd Patterson seven times in the third round of their fight*

"Joe hit Galento so hard, they could have counted him out in the air."

> *Bugs Baer, after Joe Louis knocked out Tony Galento*

"He hit me 18 times while I was going down the last time. I got a family to think about and if anybody wants to see the execution of Max Baer, he's got to pay more than $25 for a ringside seat."

> *Max Baer, on getting pummeled by Joe Louis*

"The last one up is a sissy."

> *Max Baer, after tripping while knocking down Primo Carnera*

"I'm always a slow starter. I guess I started even slower than usual."

> *Duane Bobick, on being knocked out in 58 seconds by Ken Norton*

"He trained for six months and didn't even get a chance to use his stool."

> *Curtis Cokes, on Norton's knocking out Bobick in 58 seconds*

"The battery at Yankee Stadium last night was Louis pitching, Schmeling catching."

> *Bob Considine, sportswriter, after Joe Louis thrashed Max Schmeling in their rematch, at Yankee Stadium*

"What was I supposed to do? Write him a letter?"

> *Jack Dempsey, after knocking out Jack Sharkey while Sharkey was complaining to the referee*

"I don't want to knock my opponent out. I want to hit him, step away, and watch him hurt. I want his heart."

> *Joe Frazier*

"I held on to the floor with both hands, because the ring and the audience outside were making a complete clockwise revolution, came to a stop, and went back again counterclockwise."

> *Paul Gallico, sportswriter, on being knocked out by Jack Dempsey in an exhibition match*

"You know if I fight him again, he might do the same thing to me all over again."

> *Rocky Graziano, on controlling a fight against Tony Zale and then losing by a surprise knockout*

"One of these days I think I'll get up."

> *Dave "Boy" Green, after getting knocked out by Sugar Ray Leonard*

"Everybody better get in their seats early. No Cokes, don't get no hot dogs, no nothing."

> *Marvin Hagler, predicting a quick KO of Mustafa Hamsho before knocking out Hamsho in the third round*

"Jim, if you had been paying as much attention to me as the guy out there, you wouldn't have got hit with that right."

> Tommy Loughran, after a fight
> during which a fan yelled out to Jim
> Braddock to knock Loughran out

"Nobody yells 'timber' when he unloads."

> Allan Malamud, on Evander
> Holyfield's lack of a knockout punch

"People don't come to a fight to see nice boxing. They come to see someone knocked out."

> Saoul Mamby

"The referee started to count over me. I told him, 'Don't count, go get a doctor. I'll count.'"

> Jackie Mason, on being knocked
> down as an amateur

"I thought it would never end."

> John McKay, football coach, after
> Sonny Liston knocked out Floyd
> Patterson a little more than two
> minutes into the first round

" 'Bout the time it would have taken for a tree to fall on you."

> *Archie Moore, on an exhibition with writer George Plimpton, on how long it would have taken to knock Plimpton out*

"I had a headache."

> *Archie Moore, asked how he felt after being knocked out by Cassius Clay in the fourth round*

"You're damn right I know where I am. I'm in Madison Square Garden getting beaten up."

> *Willie Pastrano, asked by the referee if he knew where he was after being knocked down by Jose Torres*

"I zigged when I should have zagged."

> *Jack Roper, on being knocked out by Joe Louis*

"Let's take a walk around the roof."

> *Eddie Sims, responding to a referee who asked if he was all right after being knocked down by Joe Louis*

"Sleep came as it must come to all British heavyweights, midway in the fifth round."

> *Red Smith, describing a knockout of British heavyweight Bruce Woodcock*

"If there was anything to learn, it was how to fall, because everybody was going down."

> *Michael Spinks, after gearing up for a fight with Larry Holmes by watching tapes of champs taking on lighter heavyweights*

"I don't want to miss the Letterman show."

> *Tony Tucker, on why he wanted to knock out Lennox Lewis in the first round*

"A boxer knocked down is the loneliest guy in the world."

> *Gene Tunney*

"I don't care nothin' about the revenge business. That never did nobody no good."

> *Jersey Joe Walcott, asked to state his feelings after knocking out Joe Louis*

SAM LANGFORD

"He hit me on the top of my head and I thought the roof had caved in."

Gunboat Jones, on the punching power of Sam Langford

LENGTHWISE

"Why? His man's not that tall."

Bugs Baer, when the manager of Rocky Marciano's opponent, Don Cockell, requested a 20-foot instead of a 16-foot ring

"He's so big, he has overcoat buttons on his fly."

Bugs Baer, on Primo Carnera

"Any heavyweight fighter who is afraid of another man shouldn't be a fighter."

James Beattie, asked if boxers were intimidated by his 6'7" height

"Six feet four."

> *Mark Breland, 6'2" fighter, when*
> *asked what he wanted to be*

"The bigger they come, the harder they fall."
> *Bob Fitzsimmons*

"You were never middleweight champ because you was too short for your height."

> *Tony Galento, on 5'4", 160-pound*
> *Danny Rubino*

"I like the big 200-pounders. You get a bigger target, and those guys don't move around too fast."

> *Harry Greb, on being 160 pounds*
> *and 5'8"*

"He is a freak. Anyone who is 6'1" should be playing basketball."

> *Marvin Hagler, on Thomas Hearns,*
> *who kept calling the 5'9" Hagler a*
> *midget*

"A fighting machine on stilts."

> *John L. Sullivan, on the tall and*
> *skinny Bob Fitzsimmons*

BENNY LEONARD

"If Leonard was hiding what they say he has lost in six years of defending his title, he is a better magician than Houdini."

> *W. O. McGeehan, sportswriter, on*
> *Benny Leonard's convincing win over*
> *Lew Tendler*

SUGAR RAY LEONARD

"This kid could feint you out of your jockstrap."

> *Angelo Dundee, on Sugar Ray*
> *Leonard*

"I'm like a diamond in the mud. They search to find ways to trap me."

> *Sugar Ray Leonard, on why his*
> *publicity outside the ring hurts his*
> *reputation inside it*

"You look at the record and you picture Hulk Hogan. You look at the fighter and it's *Leave It to Beaver*."

Jim Murray, on Sugar Ray

SONNY LISTON

"They cut him four ways—up, down, deep, and often."

Mike De John, heavyweight, on the managers of Sonny Liston

"Ever since I was born, I've been fighting for my life."

Sonny Liston

LONGEVITY

"I had more fights in one year than many of these guys have in their entire careers."

Jake LaMotta, on fighting 20 times in 1941

"They lost a few along the way, but who's counting?"

> *Archie Moore, on* Ring Encyclopedia *noting for the record that he knocked out 141 boxers in 229 bouts*

LOOK, MA, NO CAVITIES

"I fear no man but the dentist."

> *George Foreman, asked if he was intimidated by Mike Tyson*

LOSING

"If you're going to go into the tank, learn how to swim."

> *Art Aragon, on Roberto Duran's "No Mas" fight against Sugar Ray Leonard*

"It was so lonesome on my way back to the dressing room. I nearly caught cold from the draft. Just me and my trainer took the walk."

Max Baer, after losing his
heavyweight title to James J.
Braddock

"If there's a good loser in boxing, I'd love to fight him every week."

Gene Fullmer

JOE LOUIS

"As soon as the bell rang, they folded like tulips."

Ray Arcel, trainer of several different
fighters who faced Joe Louis

"I took his best punches. He has to hit you a million times before he gives you a headache."

Buddy Baer, offering a contrary view
of Louis

"Then you better keep an eye on Arthur Donovan [the ref] because somebody out there is beating the hell out of me."

> *Max Baer, on being told by trainer*
> *Jack Dempsey not to worry because*
> *Louis hadn't hit him yet*

"Like someone jammed an electric bulb in your face and busted it."

> *James J. Braddock, on Louis's jab*

"I couldn't have got up if they offered me a million dollars."

> *James J. Braddock, on being knocked*
> *out by Louis*

"He's a credit to his race—the human race."

> *Jimmy Cannon, on Joe Louis*

"He ain't gentle, but he's a real gentleman."

> *Billy Conn, on Louis's letting him*
> *recover from a slip during their fight*

"When I talk about that fight, my nose still bleeds."

> *Tommy Farr, on lasting 15 tough*
> *rounds with Louis*

"This here Louis ain't the world wonder. I figure I had him in the first. I found he could be hit."

> *Tony Galento, who knocked out Louis*
> *in the first but lost the fight*

"Louis turned a brawny, courageous man into a babbling, goggle-eyed jelly."

> *Paul Gallico, on Louis's dispatching*
> *Primo Carnera in six rounds*

"Louis is too good to be true, and he is absolutely true."

> *Ernest Hemingway*

"Up from the ghetto of Detroit rose a young David who slew Hitler's Goliath."

> *Jesse Jackson, on the significance of*
> *Louis's victory over Schmeling in*
> *their second fight*

"I was born in 1941 and my name is Jesse Louis Jackson."

> *Jesse Jackson, on the significance*
> *Louis had to his family*

"God, how the man can punch."

> *Johnny Paycheck, on being knocked*
> *out by Louis*

LOUIS—CONN I

"He can't box a lick. He has to hit you with those punches to hurt you, and he couldn't hit me in the britches with a bull fiddle."

> *Billy Conn, before facing Louis*

"Man, I loaned you my title for 12 rounds and you couldn't keep it."

> *Joe Louis, losing badly to Conn*
> *before knocking him out in the 13th*
> *round*

"How many cigars you swallow, John?"

> *Joe Louis, to John Roxborough,*
> *Louis's manager, during a fight in*
> *which Louis struggled before winning*
> *in a knockout*

LOVE AND ROMANCE

"Not with anybody else."

> *Muhammad Ali, asked if he was ever*
> *in love*

"Sports' most notorious playboy since Secretariat went to stud."

> *Dave Anderson, on Ali*

"It's not like you just go for it once and forget about it. If it's right there in front of you and you go once, you're gonna go for it again."

> *Freddie Brown, longtime trainer, on*
> *sex before a fight*

"Whenever a guy comes to me and talks about his wife or girlfriend, I say, 'Look, do me a favor, go hit the light bag.'"

Angelo Dundee

"I usually take them to the fights. I get free passes."

Charlie Goldman, Rocky Marciano's longtime trainer, on his dates

"Pinochle is the safest game between workouts."

A. J. Liebling, elaborating on his recommendation that boxers not do any other outside activities during training

MAIL CALL

"I just wanted to get them in the mail before the postage goes up."

Lou Nova, heavyweight fighter, on mailing postcards to sportswriters across the country for the heck of it

MALAPROPS AND FRACTURED SYNTAX

"When I see things through my eyes, I see things."
Angelo Dundee

"I liked Chicago. They trut me good."
Rocky Graziano

"Congratulations, you have a great future behind you."
Marvin Hagler, to James "Quick" Tillis

"I want to go down in immortality."
Larry Holmes, on why he wanted to break Rocky Marciano's undefeated record

"Boxing is ruined by TV and amachoos."
Jack Hurley, longtime promoter

"I should have stood in bed."

> *Joe Jacobs, Max Schmeling's manager, after going to a World Series game in 1934 played in subfreezing temperatures*

"It's what you call Plutonic."

> *Don King, on his relationship with Robin Givens*

"He's got a whole new set of banisters."

> *Don King, on Mike Tyson's hiring a new group of attorneys*

"This kid used to be amateur champion of the whole British umpire."

> *Jake Mintz, trainer, on middleweight Wilf Greaves*

"I never seed anything like it."

> *Tex Rickard, on 80,000 people showing up for a Dempsey–Carpentier fight*

"I'll have a well-to-do steak."

> *Maxie Rosenbloom*

"You think I'm gonna take a chance and let the guy hit me so I could get a conclusion of the brain or something?"

> *Maxie Rosenbloom, after being urged by his trainer to go out and fight*

"Page controlled the temple of this fight."

> *Renaldo Snipes, on a Greg Page–Larry Frazier fight*

"He lived to fight. Even if he didn't get paid for it, he'd still want a fight just to release the monopoly."

> *Chick Wergeles, on Beau Jack*

"He makes a good interview on account of his Southern brawl."

> *Chick Wergeles, on Beau Jack*

"He went in on account of he wanted to. He wasn't grafted or nothing."

> *Chick Wergeles, on Beau Jack's joining the Army*

MANAGERS

"Never have so few taken so much from so many."
Saoul Mamby, on managers

"Show me a fight manager with money and I'll show you the luckiest guy in the world."
Tex Sullivan, longtime manager

ROCKY MARCIANO

"He hits you with something that looks like a little tap to the crowd, but the guy who gets it shakes right down to his legs."
Fred Brown, on Rocky Marciano

"Rocky Marciano stood out like a rose in a garbage dump."
Jimmy Cannon

"A man of gentleness, kindness, compassion, and affability who brought dignity to the championship he held with such modest graciousness."

> *Arthur Daley, sportswriter, on*
> *Marciano*

"If Marciano's jaw isn't made of iron, it's at least made of poured concrete."

> *Arthur Daley*

"He goes in for a fight like I go in for a glass of beer."

> *Charlie Goldman, his trainer, on*
> *Marciano's never being fazed by an*
> *opponent*

"He must be good. He always beats the other fella."

> *Charley Goldman*

"Rocky was addicted to exercise as some men are addicted to the bottle."

> *Frank Graham, sportswriter*

"After a fight with Marciano, you felt like someone had been beating you all over the upper body with a blackjack or hitting you with rocks."

Archie Moore

"A right hand that registered nine on the Richter scale."

Red Smith

MARITAL HARMONY

"I won't worry about who you sleep with if you won't worry about who sleeps with me."

Muhammad Ali, responding to the constant attention being focused on his love life

"My toughest fight was with my first wife."

Muhammad Ali

"I was booed every time I fought. Nobody really hated me, though, except my four ex-wives."

Art Aragon

"My wife don't care that I do what I like. I'm the one taking the punches."

Lou Bizarro, before a fight against Roberto Duran

"The fact is that when I marry, it will mean the end of my career in the ring. The two don't go together."

Jack Dempsey

"In time, she'll get him. You can be dethroned in your own home. . . . Tyson thinks he's 5'11", but she can make him 2'11"."

George Foreman, on Robin Givens's marriage to Mike Tyson

"No, I'm living à la carte."

Charlie Goldman, asked if he was married

"I never hated anyone. The only one I disliked was Leon Spinks. He made a pass at my wife."

Larry Holmes

"We almost got married."

Jake LaMotta, on fighting Sugar Ray Robinson six times

"She always complained she didn't have anything to wear. I never believed her until I saw her pictures in *Playboy*."

Jake LaMotta, on one of his ex-wives

"In my whole career, I've never really gotten hurt. The only ones that really hurt me were my wives."

Jake LaMotta

"She said I clashed with the drapes."

Jake LaMotta, on why his first wife left him

"I don't care when he comes home. He still has to throw out the garbage."

Sandy LeDoux, wife of heavyweight Scott, asked if she was concerned about groupies

"I don't mind if he [Cassius Clay] beats my husband as long as he leaves me a little bit."

Veronica London, wife of British heavyweight Brian London

"I got married so I could concentrate on boxing."

Elisha Obed, junior middleweight

"Three of my wives were very good housekeepers. After we got divorced, they kept the house."

Willie Pep

"I've got it made. I've got a wife and a TV, and they're both working."

Willie Pep

"After six years, I finally got a divorce. I didn't feel at home with her. My wife had so many books in the house, whenever I came in, I had to show her a library card."

Maxie Rosenbloom, on being married to a psychologist

"I had just got married. We were just two kids in love and didn't know that this was no way to get ready to enter the ring, where you need all the energy you can get."

Jack Sharkey, on why he was
knocked out by an obscure fighter

"It's like putting a Volkswagen into the Indy 500."
Ron Standler's wife, on Standler's
facing Joe Frazier

"Wives hurt fighters. When it's right for you to marry—I'll tell you."
Al Weill, Rocky Marciano's manager,
to the boxer

MARQUESS OF QUEENSBURY

"Beer mugs, knees, fists, elbows, and the top of your head take the place of the Marquess of Queensbury rules."
Tex Cobb, on fighting

"Who is this guy Queensbury? I don't see anything wrong in sticking your thumb into my guy's eye. Just a little."

Tony Galento

MEDIOCRITY

"The Joe Blows. How can a fighter get up for them? Look at the record: Blue Lewis. I looked bad. Cooper. I looked bad. Wepner. I looked bad. Evangelista. I looked bad."

Muhammad Ali, on his having
problems against mediocre fighters

"As a matchmaker, I'd never have booked myself. I was a stinker."

Mickey Duff, legendary British
promoter/manager and a former
boxer

"My brief career as a pug was so condensed, it was engraved on a pinhead—mine."

Bob Hope

"For me the chance to fight Patterson was a fantastic opportunity. But boxing had to be in a sorry state to allow it to happen."

Pete Rademacher, on his mediocrity

"I think I escaped relatively unscathed, thanks to my scientific boxing techniques."

Chuck Wepner, poking fun at himself after being mauled by Sonny Liston

MEMBERS OF THE PRESS

"I'm the best friend a reporter ever had, because I always give good quotes, changing them around so everyone gets a fresh one."

Cassius Clay

"You see, my newspaper articles are written by a ghostwriter who makes up his own mind as to who will win and who will lose and then proceeds to make the pick under my signature."

James Corbett, who had a postfight career as sportswriter, defending himself from critics who claimed he was a lousy fight predictor

"If punches weren't being thrown, I'd describe the body movements, the footwork, and that seemed to create excitement for listeners."

Don Dunphy, boxing announcer, on creating excitement in broadcasts

"What made George Foreman was the writers. They tell people about you. Without those guys, you're dead. One thing, though—they lied about my waistline."

George Foreman

"In the old days they used to have good fight writers. That Damon Runyon, before he went on the wagon, could lay on the floor and write better than most of these guys."

Doc Kearns

"These newspapermen ask dumb questions. They'll look up at the sun and ask you if the sun is shining."

Sonny Liston

"When I was doing New York and New Jersey fight shows in the 1930s, $1,500 was a huge gate. For this fight, just returning writers' phone calls—my phone bills alone will be $1,500."

> *Irving Rudd, publicist for the*
> *Leonard–Hagler fight*

"That's the reason most of you newspapermen have a complexion like a banana. You haven't many brains, or you wouldn't be smoking."

> *John L. Sullivan, chastising a*
> *reporter for smoking while*
> *interviewing him*

MICE OR MEN

"Larry Holmes has the courage of a mouse."

> *Bob Arum*

MIRROR, MIRROR ON THE WALL

"I'm the prettiest thing that ever put on boxing gloves."

Muhammad Ali

"Boxing's a rough sport. After every fight I rush to the mirror to make sure I'm presentable."

Muhammad Ali

"I'm so beautiful, I should be chiseled in gold."

Muhammad Ali

"I want to win as badly as anyone, but it's just as important to me that I protect myself. When I'm through fighting, I don't want my children to be ashamed of how I look."

Curtis Cokes, welterweight champion

"I was looking at the TV screen. I have a photo shoot tomorrow."

Oscar De La Hoya, asked why he was looking up at the top of the stadium during his fight against John Molina

"Certainly not. I think of myself as very, very handsome."

> *Salvador Sanchez, featherweight champ, asked if he thought he was handsome*

MR. SANDMAN

"I was asleep between rounds, and I wasn't doing too well during the rounds, either."

> *Art Aragon, on taking a sleeping pill by mistake before a fight*

MR. T

"If you cross Mr. T, they say he'll dot both your eyes."

> *Skip Bayless, sportswriter, on the early days of Mr. T as Leon Spinks's bodyguard*

MONEY MAKES THE
WORLD GO 'ROUND

"Don't ever say no until you hear the price."
Pete Ashlock, boxing promoter

"Not yet. I still have the million to get."
Max Baer, asked if his name was
Maximillian

"When I made it, I spent it. Sometimes I spent it
faster than I made it."
Max Baer

"I got two dollars and a half for my first fight. My
manager gave me 50 cents and when I complained,
he said, 'Forget it, kid. You lost the fight, and
besides, you had something to eat.'"
Billy Conn

"For two million, I'd fight an old lady with a
kickstand—nothing personal."
Bobby Czyz

"When you're fighting, you're fighting for one thing: to get money."
Jack Dempsey

"Thank God, I can help everybody who needs it."
Roberto Duran, on the money he made in boxing

"You write that and I'll make a bagful of money in the rematch. I'll be so rich that bankers will come to me and say, 'George, lend us some money.'"
George Foreman, after several writers claimed he lost to Axel Schulz

"I've found out it's a lot easier to get work if you already have money than if you don't. I guess that's because people figure maybe you can do something for them in return."
Rocky Graziano

"I was an awful chump with the first money I got for fightin'. I couldn't wait to get back over to the old neighborhood to start spendin' it around with my pals."
Rocky Graziano

"He's got it made. He put his money in four banks—Aqueduct, Belmont, Roosevelt, and Yonkers Raceway."

> *Rocky Graziano, on a former champ*

"I'm a cheap imitation of Muhammad Ali, because I'm broke."

> *Larry Holmes, early in his career, on his 19–0 record*

"I figured Burns had something coming to him. I certainly wished to give him his $35,000 worth."

> *Jack Johnson, after toying with Tommy Burns during their 14-round fight*

"Those checks may be all right, but they don't look so good to this baby as those bills with big numbers on them."

> *Jack Johnson, who picked Tex Rickard to promote his fight with Jim Jeffries because Rickard outbidded other promoters with cash*

"Fight me and make a lot of money."

> *Sugar Ray Leonard, asked to think of a suitable epitaph for himself*

"When the check clears."

> *Sugar Ray Leonard, asked when the*
> *pain goes away after a fight*

"They say that money talks, but the only thing it ever said to me was good-bye."

> *Joe Louis*

"I ain't broke. I ain't rich, but I make enough to take care of my family. I never did need much money. It was always those people around me who did."

> *Joe Louis*

"Hell, for that money, Spinks will come to your house."

> *Ferdie Pacheco, on tapes of the*
> *Ali–Spinks fights selling for $90*

"I got a roomful of trophies. I want a purse."

> *Willie Pep, on why he wanted $1,000*
> *in lieu of a trophy for being inducted*
> *into the Connecticut Sports Hall of*
> *Fame*

"There's been more dough blown on fighters than was ever made off them."

Charley Rose

"Dempsey hit me harder 'cause he hit me for $300,000. Now, Joe Louis only hit me for $30,000."

Jack Sharkey, asked to compare Jack Dempsey with Joe Louis

"He's all right as long as he can walk to the bank."

Bill Slayton, Ken Norton's trainer, after Norton lost to Gerry Cooney in a first-round knockout

"I'll fight him for nothing if the price is right."

Marlon Starling, on an opponent he was not too fond of

ARCHIE MOORE

"Is there anybody in the world who doesn't like Moore? If I can find the guy I'll charge admission, because he must be one in 10 million."

> *Dan Florio, trainer, on the popularity*
> *of Archie Moore*

"Moore is of the same professional age as an attorney who has practiced for 125 years."

> *A. J. Liebling, on Moore's 25-year*
> *boxing career*

NAME GAME

"The next time we fight, I'm going to knock the 'a' out of him and he'll be Sad Muhammad."

> *Dwight Braxton, on a rematch with*
> *Matthew Saad Muhammad*

"When I get through, you're going to be Jimmy Old and not Jimmy Young."

> *Michael Dokes, to Jimmy Young*
> *before they fought*

"I called them Gus and Andy."

> *Don Dunphy, boxing announcer, on*
> *how he handled a fight between Gus*
> *Lesnevich and Anton Christoforidis*

"Richard officially changed his name to All Dunn."

> *John Hall, sportswriter, after Richard*
> *Dunn lost to Ali in five rounds*

"When I get done with Sweet Pea, he'll be Split Pea."

> *Greg Haugan, on fighting Pernell*
> *"Sweet Pea" Whitaker*

"It'll be a winner-take-all fight, the winner to take permanent possession of the name Sugar Ray."

> *Sugar Ray Seales, on wanting to*
> *fight Sugar Ray Leonard*

NERVES

"If a lion ain't scared, you can pull his tail and tweak his nose and ride on him and he'll yawn. But if he's scared, God help you."

> *Eddie "Cannonball" Brown, trainer, on why he believes a fighter should go into the ring scared*

"Why the hell should I be? Ain't I gonna be fighting in a few minutes?"

> *Harry Greb, asked if he was nervous before a fight*

"Fear was absolutely necessary. Without it, I would have been scared to death."

> *Floyd Patterson, on the secret of success*

KEN NORTON

"I'd like to get a steamroller and lay Norton down and crush him flat. Other than that, I like him."

> *George Foreman*

"Look at all that jewelry he wears. Who does he think he is, Sammy Davis Jr.? . . . He can't fight; he's nothing but an experienced amateur."
Jimmy Young, on Norton

NOSEDIVE

"I could pass a fish factory and never know the difference."
Art Aragon, on boxing wrecking his sense of smell

"I had 27 sinus operations and now they say you shouldn't have any. That's how they found out."
Jack Hurley, fight manager

NUMBERS GAME

"People live their lives by numbers. They say, 'Oh, I'm 80! I better go off somewhere and die.' Numbers are for accountants."
George Foreman

"Was that too long?"

> *Amos Johnson, on taking 14 seconds
> to get back into the ring after being
> knocked over the ropes by Ray
> Staples*

"I have never been more than 70 percent of myself.
My ambition is to be 100 percent."

> *Floyd Patterson*

"How many guesses do I get?"

> *Chuck Wepner, after being knocked
> down in the ninth round of a fight
> against Liston and being asked by
> the referee how many fingers he had*

OCCUPATIONAL HAZARDS

"Breathing those chemicals, I could have died
faster than in the ring."

> *Michael Spinks, who quit work at a
> chemical factory to fight
> professionally*

OLD DAYS

"Because they're lazy."
> *Beau Jack, on why fighters don't take on as many fights as they did in the old days*

"It always turns out to be the time when he was fighting."
> *A. J. Liebling, on a retired boxer's definition of the sport's "glory days"*

"Somewhere between nostalgia and neuralgia, everything old becomes new again."
> *Robert Lipsyte, New York Times columnist, on old-timers in boxing*

OLYMPICS

"That's like batting .400 in the minor leagues."
> *Riddick Bowe, after Lennox Lewis beat him in the 1988 Olympics*

ON THE RUN

"Every time you do, it shortens your career. The public likes a fearless slugger, but that won't pay your hospital bills."

> *Willie Pep, advising Willie Pastrano*
> *not to get hit*

"He who fights and runs away, lives to fight another day."

> *Willie Pep*

OPPONENTS

"It doesn't make any difference to me. Some washerwoman. . . . Some SOB in shorts and gloves."

> *Tex Cobb, on not caring about who*
> *his opponent is*

"The only way you could beat me would be if I had both arms and both legs cut off, and I lost my vision."

> *Howard Davis, before fighting*
> *Termite Watkins*

"An opponent is a fella that is always dependable, that can give a good account of himself and lose."
> *Chris Dundee*

"Why, I knocked him out the other day while I was shadowboxing in my room and he was 200 miles away."

> *Sonny Liston, asked if he was*
> *concerned about fighting Brian*
> *London*

"The spareribs will be tougher than Cooney's opponents."

> *Barney Nagler, sportswriter, on a*
> *dinner for Gerry Cooney*

PAIN

"I hate to say it, but it's true that I only like it better when pain comes."
>*Frank "The Animal" Fletcher*

"I don't like to get hit. You know why? It hurts."
>*Willie Pastrano, on his adroitness at ducking punches*

PARTY ON

"Tony caused more delays in the service than the Otis Elevator repairman could handle."
>*Ray Arcel, on good-looking welterweight Tony Janiro, who met an attractive elevator operator at a hotel where Arcel and Janiro were staying*

"Well, two out of three ain't bad."
>*Max Baer, on wasting his life on wine, women, and song*

"I struck a blow against clean living."

Jack Dempsey, on beating clean-cut
Homer Smith

"Until the day I was champion, I was hungry. Then, after I won, I start to do bad things."

Ingemar Johansson, on his playboy
reputation

"If this doesn't motivate Tommy [Morrison] to keep away from the booze and women for the next six months, nothing will."

Tommy Virgets, Morrison's trainer, on
Lennox Lewis's unimpressive win
against Frank Bruno

FLOYD PATTERSON

"Before he fights me again, he'd rather run through hell in a gasoline sports coat."

Cassius Clay

"I'll beat him so bad, he'll need a shoehorn to put his hat on."

Cassius Clay

"He knocks you down, he wants to pick you up."

> *Dan Florio, trainer of Patterson, on why Patterson is too nice a guy for the fight game*

PAY-PER-VIEW

"He is listed on pay-per-view as what's-his-name."

> *Jim Murray, on the obscurity of heavyweight champ Oliver McCall*

"We've got filet mignon versus Gainesburger."

> *Rock Newman, on the pay-per-view war between Bowe–Holyfield and Tyson–Mathis Jr., before it was agreed that Tyson would fight on Fox*

WILLIE PEP

"Trying to hit Pep is like trying to step on a flame."

> *Kid Campeche*

"He was so clever, he could come up to an opponent from behind."

> *Don Dunphy*

"At least I can always tell people I once fought Willie Pep."

> *Jackie Lennon, on the bright side of losing to Pep*

"The longer he goes, the more astonishing he becomes."

> *Red Smith*

PHONE IT IN

"My guy would have won if they fought in a phone booth."

> *Angelo Dundee, Ali's trainer, after being accused of loosening ropes in the Ali–Foreman fight*

"Let's do it over the phone."

> *Larry Holmes, on Tex Cobb's suggestion that they fight again in a phone booth*

"If boxing matches were held in telephone booths, I'd be the champion."

Chuck Wepner

POETRY IN MOTION

"Float like a butterfly, sting like a bee. If you ain't for Big Jim, you'll reckon with me."

Muhammad Ali, on the campaign trail for Illinois governor James Thompson

"The Cat and me will take care of Clay in three."

Hugh Benbow, trainer of Cleveland "The Cat" Williams

"That's no jive. Cooper will fall in five."

Cassius Clay, whose prediction came true when he knocked out Henry Cooper in the fifth round

"I'm gonna do to Buster what the Indians did to Custer."

Cassius Clay, on fighting Buster Mathis

"Jones likes to mix, so I'll let it go six. If he's talking jive, I'll let it go in five. And if he talks some more, I'll cut it to four."

Cassius Clay, on fighting Doug Jones,
who went the distance

"To aggravate and nauseate."

Cassius Clay, on his style against
Cleveland Williams

"They must fall in the round I call."

Cassius Clay

"Before you bet your money, remember what happened to Sonny."

Cassius Clay, on fighting Floyd
Patterson after beating Liston

"He will go in eight, and if he keeps talking jive, he will go in five."

Cassius Clay, before his first fight
with Liston

"I'd throw in the towel before I'd faint at the Liston scowl."

> *Cassius Clay, before his first fight with Liston*

"After I beat the bear [Liston], I'll go after the hare [Patterson]."

> *Cassius Clay, referring to the nicknames for Sonny Liston ("the Black Bear") and Floyd Patterson ("the Rabbit")*

"When you come to the fight, don't block the aisles. And don't block the door, for you may all go home after Round 4."

> *Cassius Clay, before fighting Archie Moore, whom he knocked out in the fourth round*

"He was old and I was new. And you could tell by the blows I threw. I swept that old man clean out of the ring, for a new broom sweeps 'most anything."

> *Cassius Clay, after fighting Archie Moore*

"Liston was hungry, rough, and tough, while the champ had already had enough. As the people left the park you could hear them say, 'Liston will be champ until he meets Clay.'"

Cassius Clay, after Sonny Liston knocked out Floyd Patterson

"Some say the greatest was Sugar Ray, but they have not seen Cassius Clay."

Cassius Clay, on Sugar Ray Robinson

"If he had stayed in Sweden, he wouldn't have taken that beatin'."

Cassius Clay, after the third Floyd Patterson–Ingemar Johansson fight, won easily by Patterson

"Vito the Mosquito, I'll swat him like a fly."

Marvin Hagler, on Vito Antuofermo

"The fat man will be in motion and it will be poetry. You will see unity of fatness in motion in the proper fashion."

Leroy Jones, 255-pounder, before fighting Larry Holmes for the heavyweight title

"So that the President will be safe from getting shot."

> *Muhammad Ali, explaining why he*
> *had ambitions to be Vice President*

"At least as honest as our political system."

> *Tex Cobb, on boxing's bizarre*
> *ranking system*

"I also voted for McGovern and Mondale."

> *Billy Crystal, on picking Michael*
> *Spinks to beat Mike Tyson*

"Whenever you order a banana split, they never give you the whole banana. If I'm elected, there'll be a whole banana in every split."

> *George Foreman, on running for*
> *President on a split ticket*

"It's like meeting Santa Claus. You go in, shake his hand, have your picture taken, and then you leave."

> *Ray Mancini, on meeting President*
> *Reagan*

"I will take the examination to test for brain damage if you will."

> *Archie Moore, after a member of*
> *Parliament urged that every boxer be*
> *given a test for brain damage*

"Coetzer belongs in the Top 10. But moving him to No. 1 must have taken some quintessential politicians."

> *Rock Newman, on Pierre Coetzer's*
> *facing Riddick Bowe*

"It isn't the first time."

> *Sargent Shriver, former vice-*
> *presidential candidate and friend*
> *of George Foreman, when asked*
> *how he felt about being ignored*
> *after reporters left his side to run*
> *to Foreman, who had just beaten*
> *Joe Frazier*

"I told the voters that after I finished speaking, we would show fight pictures. They had to stay and listen to me to see the movies. They stayed."

> *John Tunney, son of Gene Tunney, while running for Congress and getting huge crowds for his rallies— many of them people who wanted to see films of his father and Jack Dempsey fighting*

POOR

"Dempsey must have learned to box just trying to get a little elbow room."

> *Anonymous, at a parade for Jack Dempsey that passed by the cabin where he grew up*

"I grew up in an alley. I never saw a street till I was 18 years old."

> *Billy Conn, asked if he was a street kid*

"Snapshots? Hell, I never even owned a pair of shoes until I was 12 years old."

> *Jack Dempsey, asked by someone if he had any snapshots of himself as a child*

"You could hit me on the chin with a sledgehammer. When you haven't eaten for two days, you'll understand."

> *Jack Dempsey*

"When I was a kid in Houston, we were so poor we couldn't afford the last two letters, so we called ourselves po'."

> *George Foreman*

"We were so poor that my old man would go outside every Christmas and shoot his gun, then come back and tell us that Santa Claus had committed suicide."

> *Jake LaMotta*

PRE-FIGHT HYPE

"Let's get ready to rumble."

Michael Buffer, boxing announcer

PRISON

"He didn't go to Princeton for three years, he went to prison."

*Dan Duva, on the stupidity of Mike
Tyson's re-signing with Don King
after leaving prison*

"Because nobody will walk out in the middle of my speech."

*Marvin Hagler, on why he likes
speaking at prisons*

"Prison was the best thing that ever happened to me. I went in with a pistol and came out with an atom bomb."

*Don King, on educating himself in
prison*

"Making the best of what we had to work with."
Don King, on what boxing was like before Tyson's release from prison

"No one ever told me that—to my face, of course."
Mike Tyson, on claims that his skills eroded while he was in prison

PRO WRESTLING

"The only sport that suffers from a greater credibility problem is professional wrestling."
Seth Abraham, HBO Sports, on boxing

"It all proved boxers are so superior to rasslers. He didn't stand up and fight like a man."
Muhammad Ali, after fighting Japanese wrestler Antonio Inoki

"No, I think pro wrestling should be handled by the Theater Guild."
Anthony Felice, WBA bigwig, asked if pro wrestling and boxing should be within the same organization

"I am applying special training to strengthen it. I have people step on my chin and knead it with their shoes."

> *Antonio Inoki, on strengthening his chin for a match with Ali*

"It beats stealin'."

> *Joe Louis, on his days in professional wrestling*

PROMOTERS

"I'd say I was a no-good sorry SOB, but if I was better-educated, I'd do better."

> *Pete Ashlock, promoter, on self-assessment*

"I have never been around so many crummy people in all my life."

> *Ed "Too Tall" Jones, on promoters*

"There have only been three really great promoters in our lifetime. There's Michael Todd, P. T. Barnum, and yours truly."

> *Don King*

"I must go where the wild goose goes."

Don King, on why he promotes so many top fighters

"To maintain a sense of proportion, it is well to remember that one does not mention rope in the house of a hangman or speak of compassion in the presence of a fight promoter."

Barney Nagler, sportswriter

"I wear their abhorrence as a badge of honor. . . . If I ever felt like I was accepted, I'd go take a shower."

Rock Newman, on being hated by Bob Arum and Don King

"Give the people what they want, the way they want it, and not the way you think best."

Tex Rickard, on the keys to successful promotion

"Sit behind a desk, smoke a big cigar, and drink whiskey all night."

Mike Rossman, on his view of promoters

"In what other business would the likes of Arum and King be the pinnacle? If those two guys are the sharpest guys in the business, what does that tell you about everybody else?"

> *Mike Trainer, Sugar Ray Leonard's attorney*

PUNCHING POWER

"This was a new experience to me. I'm used to putting people to sleep with my punch."

> *Roger Andersson, Swedish heavyweight who revived a man who had fainted by hitting him*

"If you get belted and see three fighters through a haze, go after the one in the middle. That's what ruined me—going after the other two guys."

> *Max Baer*

"Don King makes Mike Tyson out to be Superman, but I've got the Kryptonite, right here."

> *Frank Bruno, pointing to his right fist*

"Nobody hits harder than Shavers. If somebody did, I'd shoot him."

Tex Cobb, on Earnie Shavers

"He ain't gonna make no grown man cry, but it was a good boxing lesson."

Tex Cobb, on the punching power of Larry Holmes

"Keep punching."

Jack Dempsey, giving advice to aspiring boxers

"I've missed a guy and seen him cower down and just about say thank you. Even when I look bad, I am hurting people. Even when I miss, they suffer."

George Foreman, on his punch

"I wouldn't trade stamps with him."

Joey Giardello, asked if he would trade punches with Dick Tiger

"He doesn't jab you. He two-by-fours you."
Pinkie Green, on the punching power of Cleveland Williams

"The punch you throw will take care of itself. It's the next one you gotta have ready."
Charlie Goldman

"It's the shortcut to the money."
Charlie Goldman, on the punch in boxing

"I could tell he was a hard hitter by the wind he kicked up when he missed."
Sugar Hart, after saying that Rocky Kalingo was the best puncher he ever faced even though he didn't get hit

"When Earnie Shavers hit me, I thought people were taking my picture."
Larry Holmes

"Naw, I didn't use plaster of paris on the bandages. It was cement."

> *Doc Kearns, on charges that he loaded up Jack Dempsey's hands with an illegal substance for a fight with Jesse Willard*

"We threw punches that would have rocked a volcano."

> *Sugar Ray Leonard, after a fight with Wilfred Benitez*

"Man, they all hurt."

> *Archie Moore, asked what punch did the most damage after he lost to Rocky Marciano*

"[Jimmy] Young paralyzed the left side of my face and [Trevor] Berbick the right. This is not what I had in mind when I started boxing."

> *Gordie Racette*

"To hell with this, I'm boxing this guy from here on in."

> *Sugar Ray Robinson, after giving Kid Gavilan his best shot, which failed to knock The Kid down*

"It's the punch you don't see coming that hurts."
Sugar Ray Robinson

"I want to drive a man's nose bone into his brain."
*Mike Tyson, on what he wants to do
with his punches*

"I was throwing, what can you say, hydrogen
bombs. Every punch with murderous intentions."
Mike Tyson

"The last one."
*Bruce Woodcock, after being knocked
out by Tami Mauriello, when asked
which punch was the worst*

REACH ADVANTAGE

"That's only important at a boardinghouse dinner."
*Jim Murray, on reach advantage in a
fight*

REFEREES

"The referee hit me more than Duran did. The referee couldn't speak English, so he kept hitting me on the forehead to get my attention."

> *Emile Griffith, after beating Juan Duran*

"I carry my own referee."

> *Sam Langford, pointing to his fist, when asked why he was unconcerned about referees in a fight*

RELATIONSHIPS

"We have a marriage, like a father and son."

> *Don King, on his relationship with Julio Cesar Chavez*

"There's nothing I wouldn't do for him and there's nothing he wouldn't do for me, and that's how it's been for 10 years now—we've done nothing for each other."

Irving Rudd, Tommy Hearns's publicist

RELIGION

"I fear Allah, thunderstorms, and bad airplane rides."

Muhammad Ali, on his fears

"Man we're going to be blessed now. Hangin' out with the pope."

Riddick Bowe, during a trip to the Vatican

"The Lord is always good to an honest gambler."

William Brady, manager of James J. Corbett

"I don't care what religion he is. If he doesn't get moving, he's gonna lose the fight."

> *Gil Clancy, after being told Howard Davis was a vegetarian*

"I can't take off my shirt and go into the ring and hit somebody. The only time I could fight would be if somebody tried to mug me. I had boxing. This [preaching] is better."

> *George Foreman, in 1981*

"If a fighter doesn't have it, only God can help him."

> *Eddie Futch*

"Wait a minute, I gotta consult my rabbi first."

> *Irving Rudd, on his aorta being replaced by a pig's bladder*

"I don't fear anybody but God. Another boxer might knock you down, but God can do something permanent to you."

> *John Tate*

"I don't care who I'm fighting. I don't care if it's God. If I don't want God to hit me, he's not going to hit me."

Pernell Whitaker

REMATCH

"For him to talk rematch, there's more brain damage than I thought."

Sugar Ray Leonard, on Tommy Hearns's requesting a rematch

"In a return match, it is always possible that there has occurred, subsequent or consequent to the first encounter, a change in the emotional relationship of the two principals."

A. J. Liebling

RETIREMENT

"Horses get old, cars get old, the pyramids of Egypt are crumbling."

> *Muhammad Ali, on retiring from the ring for the first time at age 33*

"We change our minds so much. Look at all the divorces. Everybody says they'll marry 'til death and they're divorced a few weeks later."

> *Muhammad Ali, on retiring and then unretiring*

"All of us boxing people realize evening is here and night will soon befall us."

> *Muhammad Ali, on nearing the end of his career*

"I'm not a boxer. I'm only going to do this once."

> *Randy Cross, upon retiring from pro football*

"Farewell. Farewell to the ring and the gloves and a career which provided one big result. I almost got the title, and I hurt Dempsey badly."

> *Luis Firpo, announcing his retirement*

"I miss being punched. Seriously, I really loved the art of boxing."

> *Marvin Hagler, on retirement*

"I am not of the '90s."

> *Sugar Ray Leonard, on losing a bout with Terry Norris in 1991*

"I eat less, weigh less, train less, and care less."

> *Ray Mancini, on his retirement*

"I never retired. I just changed procedures."

> *Archie Moore*

"My opinion is to get out while you have all your brains all together and your money, and as, Joe Bugner puts it, the ability to count it."

> *Ferdie Pacheco*

"I wanted to quit while I was on top, but you cannot choose your endings."

> *Sugar Ray Robinson*

"You always say, 'I'll quit when I start to slide,' and then one morning you wake up and you've done slid."

Sugar Ray Robinson

"The punches you used to throw without thinkin', you now have to reason."

Sugar Ray Robinson, on when it's time to retire

TEX RICKARD

"[Tex had the] nerves of a guy who would bet it all on the color of the next cow."

Jim Murray, on the longtime promoter

RINGSIDE SEATS

"I once said about a fight with a $1,000 ringside seat that the people pricing the tickets must be crazy. But I'd pay $1,000 to watch this fight."

Sugar Ray Leonard, on his fight with Thomas Hearns

ROADWORK

"You can map out a fight plan or a life plan, but when the action starts, it may not go the way you planned, and you're down to your reflexes, which means your training. That's where your roadwork shows."

Joe Frazier

"His roadwork was done on the dance floor."

John Kieran, sportswriter, on Maxie Rosenbloom

"I want to invent a roadwork pill. You get up in the morning, you take the pill, have breakfast, then a deep breath, and look around and you've done five miles on the road."

Willie Pastrano

SUGAR RAY ROBINSON

"When God rang the bell and ended the fight, the world cried out for one more round."

Jesse Jackson, eulogizing Sugar Ray Robinson

"I fought Sugar Ray Robinson so many times, it's a wonder I didn't get diabetes."

Jake LaMotta

"It wasn't a fight, it was a ballet. If Nureyev was a fighter, he would do it this way."

Jim Murray, on a typical Robinson fight

"I didn't dance. I wanted him to tire, to lose power. I decided to use the ropes. He punched like a sissy."

> *Muhammad Ali, explaining his famous rope-a-dope strategy against Foreman*

"The bull is stronger, but the matador is smarter."

> *Muhammad Ali, on punishing Foreman after a rope-a-dope display*

"Then I'll show you a dope on the rope."

> *Larry Holmes, asked what would happen if Ali used rope-a-dope on him*

"I'll just hit him a couple of times and then go over and lean on another rope and stare at him. It will be a staring contest."

> *Earnie Shavers, asked what would happen if Ali tried rope-a-dope on him*

"He was so good, you couldn't hit his backside with a handful of buckshot."

Cus D'Amato

"He does everything so wrong that it must be right."

Dave Shade, one of Rosenbloom's opponents

ROUND ONE

"The bell rang, and I went to the center of the ring. I threw two left jabs, a hard left hook, a right, and then an uppercut. And then Basilio came to the center of the ring."

Art Aragon, after being manhandled by Carmen Basilio

ROYALTY

"Glad to meet you, Prince. I think I've heard of you before. If you're ever in Boston, look me up."
> *John L. Sullivan, meeting the*
> *Prince of Wales (the future*
> *King Edward VII)*

RUBDOWNS

"I didn't do that. A good fighter doesn't need a rubdown and a bad fighter doesn't deserve one."
> *Charlie Goldman, asked if he gave*
> *Rocky Marciano rubdowns after*
> *workouts*

ST. PATRICK'S DAY

"I'll fight one Irishman, but I won't fight them all."
> *Larry Holmes, on turning down a*
> *March 17 fight with Gerry Cooney*

MAX SCHMELING

"No. I saw the fight."

> *Joe Louis, after being beaten by*
> *Schmeling, when asked if he wanted*
> *to see a film of the fight to prepare*
> *for the second fight*

SCHOOL DAYS

"I was always the jerk athlete who would stand up at the team meeting and say, 'If I catch anybody drinking beer I'm gonna tell the coach.'"

> *Tex Cobb, on his days as a high*
> *school football player*

"Instead of taking auto mechanics, I took home economics. But I haven't had the opportunity to sew in some time."

> *Michael Dokes, on his choice of*
> *courses in high school*

"I think sleeping was my problem in school. If school had started at four o'clock in the afternoon, I'd be a college graduate today."

George Foreman

"I never stole anything that didn't begin with 'A': A car. A truck. A purse."

Rocky Graziano, on his juvenile delinquent days

"You want to know why I'm not up in the chips like Rocky? I'll tell you why. I wasn't lucky enough to be a juvenile delinquent."

Maxie Shapiro, former lightweight, complaining about the success of Rocky Graziano

SILENCE IS GOLDEN

"He done the job the best he could and he kept his mouth shut when he had to."

Ted Bentham, longtime trainer, asked to compose his own epitaph

"Two good rules of thumb. Don't ask Henny Youngman how to throw a left hook and don't ask Evander Holyfield if he's heard any good ones lately."

> *Wallace Matthews, sportswriter, on the not particularly outgoing Holyfield*

SOCIAL SKILLS

"I don't sing, I don't dance, and I don't recite poetry like some of my colleagues, but just to prove I'm sociable I'll fight anyone in the house."

> *Rocky Marciano, during a talk to high-school students*

"It never bothers me to hit people I like."

> *Tex Cobb*

"When I'm in the ring I'm fighting for my life."

> *John Collins, middleweight, on being a good guy out of the ring*

SPARRING PARTNERS

"Joe broke my ribs when I was his sparring partner. I never told him, but he knows I was hurt, and he still didn't give me a day off."

> *Larry Holmes, on once being Joe*
> *Frazier's sparring partner*

"No. Tomorrow at 7:30."

> *Sonny Liston, asked if he was going*
> *to spar that day, the day before his*
> *fight with Floyd Patterson*

SPEED DEMON

"I'm so fast I could hit you before God gets the news."

> *Muhammad Ali*

"I'm so fast, I hit the light switch in my room and jump into my bed before my room goes dark."

> *Muhammad Ali*

"I'll be so fast that he'll think he's surrounded."

Muhammad Ali, on fighting Foreman

"I had my opponent running all over the ring, but the trouble was that he was running after me."

Anonymous

"I want to ask you one favor. For the next time we fight, will you hold still?"

Max Baer, to Tommy Loughran, who ran him all over the ring

"George has three speeds—slow, stop, and wait a minute."

Angelo Dundee, on George Foreman

"He couldn't catch a parked bus."

Larry Holmes, on Michael Spinks's foot speed

"Sometimes too much speed gets a fellow in trouble."

Joe Louis, on speedy Billy Conn's being arrested for speeding while driving

"He can run, but he can't hide."

> *Joe Louis, on how he would fight*
> *Billy Conn*

"I moved so fast that they knocked one another out."

> *Buster Mathis, on his speed in the*
> *ring against two fighters in an*
> *exhibition match*

"Riddick crosses the ring like a glacier crossing Colorado."

> *Jim Murray, on the foot speed of*
> *Riddick Bowe*

"I'm surprised people didn't try to hang their coats on him when they came in."

> *Jim Murray, on the slow Tex Cobb*

SPORTSMANSHIP

"I'll shake after I lick you."

> *James Corbett, refusing to shake*
> *hands with Bob Fitzsimmons prior to*
> *their fight*

STILLMAN'S GYM

"There were more thieves in Stillman's Gym than in the penitentiary."
Ray Arcel

"How long do you think a man with a happy face would have lasted in my old business, running a boxing gym? Managers and fighters would have borrowed me broke. When would they have paid their bills if I had been a soft touch with a big grin?"

Lou Stillman, owner of Stillman's Gym, on maintaining a grim demeanor

STREET FIGHTS

"Surprisingly enough, I was sober at the time. I also had some fights. Two of 'em I got paid for."
Tex Cobb, on what he was up to when he went to Europe after losing to Holmes

"The toughest thing to do in the ring is restrain myself. I want to knock the other guy in the groin, but I know I can't do that."
Tex Cobb

"I didn't exactly stick around to count votes."
Tex Cobb, on breaking his arm during a street fight, when asked who won the fight

"I told them there were some rainy Saturday nights they should have been with me in various saloons."
Tex Cobb, on fans who said the Larry Holmes–Tex Cobb fight was the worst slaughter they ever saw

"If the other fella tried to make it a street fight, he wouldn't be thinking and I would, because I wouldn't be street fighting."
Floyd Patterson, on street fighting in the ring

"This is the only sport in the world where two guys get paid for doing something they'd be arrested for if they got drunk and did it for nothing."

> *Mark Robson, director of the movie*
> The Champ

"A fellow with a knife is a namby-pamby, anyway. A man will set up and use his fists."

> *Gene Tunney, on tough guys fighting instead of using weapons*

STRIKE UP THE BAND

"The singin' is easy. Memorizin' the words is hard."

> *Rocky Graziano, on his singing debut*

"Instead of practicing boxing, he should have taken voice lessons so he could have yelled for help."

> *Jackie Mason, on Michael Spinks's losing to Mike Tyson in the first round*

"You have to see sharp so you won't be flat."

> *Sugar Ray Robinson, on boxing advice*

"Who'd he ever lick?"

> *Chalky Wright, boxer who was said to like classical music, when asked what he thought of Mendelssohn*

JOHN L. SULLIVAN

"Shake the hands that shook the hand of John L. Sullivan."

> *John L. Sullivan, giving the famous greeting wherever he went*

SUPERBANTAMWEIGHT

"What the hell is a superbantamweight?"

> *Sonny Werblin, after finding out that Wilfredo Gomez would be fighting for that title*

"There are no pleasures in a fight, but some of my fights have been a pleasure to win."
Muhammad Ali

"The science of boxing is to avoid getting hit, but if you do get hit, hit the other fella before he hits you again."
Jack Blackburn, Joe Louis's trainer

"You have to be taught how to fight. It's not a strength sport. It's a skill sport."
Gil Clancy

"Never allow the situation to become boring."
Riddick Bowe, on the secret of success in boxing

"I was in no hurry to land a blow, but I was determined that when I did land, it would be a blow that would make Sullivan believe that I could hit as well as he could."

> *James Corbett, regarded as having brought the technique of boxing to the fore by beating John L. Sullivan for the heavyweight title*

"I learned as a kid that no fighter has everything. Hit a fellow on the chin and if he doesn't blink, hit him in the belly. It is as simple as that."

> *Jack Dempsey*

"Kill the other guy before he kills you."

> *Jack Dempsey*

"A fighter must do two things: be good to his mother and keep his tail off the floor."

> *Chick Ferrara, Dick Tiger's manager*

"Punch up, punch down, what the hell's the difference?"

> *Tony Galento, asked about his ability to punch up*

"Boxing is the most basic and uncomplicated of athletic competition, and, at its best, achieves the status of an art form."

Reggie Gutteridge, British sportswriter

"I am a fighter who walks, talks, and thinks fighting, but I try not to look like it."

Marvin Hagler

"They used to feed Dempsey old has-beens in the last days of his training, just so he would knock them down, and it never failed to pick up his spirits."

Al Lacey, trainer, on Jack Dempsey

"Kill the body and the head will follow."

Sam Langford

"The Sweet Science is joined onto the past like a man's arm to his shoulder."

A. J. Liebling

"One day headlines, the next day bread lines."

Lenny Mancini

"Boxing is one game where you are really on your own. There are no 10 other guys helping you, and there's nothing between you and the other guy's punches but your own skin—no pads, no helmets, no masks."

> *Rocky Marciano, comparing boxing with football*

"It's not a trade show. The idea is to hit and not get hit."

> *Janks Morton, Sugar Ray Leonard's trainer, on strategy against Marvin Hagler*

"The only fundamental I ever mastered is to wade straight in and hit whatever is in front of me."
> *Mando Muniz, welterweight*

"I enjoy outthinking another man and outmanueverin' him, but I still don't like to fight."
> *Sugar Ray Robinson*

"I am here to train for a boxing contest, not a fight. I don't like fighting. Never did. But I'm free to admit I like boxing."
> *Gene Tunney*

"A great sports psychologist told me that I could intimidate people by keep hitting them in the face for three minutes."

Mike Tyson

"Anyone who says he loves this business is a guy you have to look at very carefully. There's nothin' to love about being hit on the head."

Mike Weaver

THOSE ARE FIGHTING WORDS

"Magnificent patsy."

Muhammad Ali, on George Foreman, after their fight in Zaire

"I'm embarrassed to get in the ring with this unrated duck."

Cassius Clay, early in his career before a fight against Willie Besmanoff

"Why can't they get me a real challenger?"
> *Cassius Clay, after thrashing Floyd*
> *Patterson*

"He's a big, tall, fat bum."
> *Oliver McCall, on Riddick Bowe*

"He stinks. He's got a hard jab. If he misses it, it goes off balance. . . . And as for his big punches, you can pack a lunch before they get there."
> *Ken Norton, on George Foreman*

"I don't think much of him as a fighter, but if you put him in a 40-and-over league, he'd kill everybody."
> *Mike Tyson, on George Foreman*

THRILLA IN MANILA

"I want Joe Frazier so bad, I want my fist in his nose. . . . So watch him, don't let him get hit by no car, don't let him get kidnapped, watch the water he drinks."
> *Muhammad Ali*

"It'll be a killa, a chilla, a thrilla, when I get the gorilla in Manila."

Muhammad Ali, on Joe Frazier

"I hit him with body shots that would have brought down cities."

Muhammad Ali, on the power of the punches Joe Frazier and Ali threw at each other

TIME CRUNCH

"I beg your pardon, I'm accustomed to appearing only on the main event."

Roger Donoghue, middleweight in the 1950s who, after he was dazed by a punch and was unable to state the time of day, was told by the ref that it was 9:30

TITLE BELT

"He got the title out of a trash can."
>*Riddick Bowe, on Oliver McCall's winning the title belt that Bowe threw in the garbage*

"It's a loan, not a gift."
>*Jimmy DePiano, Mike Rossman's dad, after Victor Galindez beat Rossman for the light heavyweight title*

"Look at me. I'm just a boy and I got the belt on my waist."
>*Mike Tyson, after beating Trevor Berbick at age 20 for the heavyweight title*

TOMATO CANS

"He looks for guys from Woodlawn Cemetery."
>*Al Braverman, on Greg Page*

"I certainly would like to believe that I got this chance because I've got blue eyes and I'm a great American."

> *Tex Cobb, on why he was chosen to fight Holmes*

"If I can't beat this guy, I'll quit the ring."

> *Gerrie Coetzee, on Stan Ward*

"Alfredo prepped for Holmes by trying out a loser named Joe Maye in three rounds. Maye was in a minor losing slump when he tried Alfredo. He had won only 2 of his last 31 fights."

> *Lowell Cohn, sportswriter, on Alfredo Evangelista, the next tomato can for Holmes*

"When I saw that 12–58, I thought it was his birth date."

> *Beano Cook, on Jose Resto, who was fighting Olympic gold-medal winner Howard Davis in his first pro fight*

"Of all the tomato cans, you pick one who fights back."

> *Steve Farhood, to George Foreman after Foreman fought Axel Schulz*

"I did look in Florida for an opponent, but they said Pee Wee Herman was busy."

> *George Foreman, on looking for a tomato can after fighting Michael Moorer*

"We've been trying to get Elvis. He's been dead long enough."

> *Ray Foreman, George's brother, on George's next opponent*

"An opponent who survived a worldwide search process that weeded out anyone livelier than a Joe Louis statue."

> *Richard Hoffer, sportswriter, on George Foreman's opponent, Axel Schulz*

"Ever since the dawning, somebody discovered that the way to build a fighter up was to get him someone he can beat up."

> *Hank Kaplan, boxing historian, on opponents*

"He knocks out tomato cans; he turns into one against the stars."

> *Pat Putnam, sportswriter, on Alex*
> *Stewart, who lost to Holyfield, Tyson,*
> *Foreman, and Moorer*

TRAIN TRIP

"If this is the way things are done in New York, I'm getting the first train back from here to St. Paul."

> *Kewpie Ertle, bantamweight, after*
> *witnessing a riot in New York City*
> *following a Benny Leonard fight*

TRAIN WRECK

"Once you've been in with Shavers, you can take on a freight train. It moves, but it ain't much."
> *Tex Cobb*

"You're only as good as the fighter you work with. I don't care how much you know, if your fighter can't fight, you're another bum in the park."
Ray Arcel

"My old trainer taught me one important thing. Win this fight. Look good in the next one."
George Benton, longtime trainer

"I'm only as good as the guy in the stool."
Angelo Dundee

"The era of the trainer or manager talking for the fighter is over. They're not going to do the fighting, so they shouldn't be doing the talking, either."
Sugar Ray Leonard

"You here again?"
Joe Louis, to Ray Arcel, who faced Louis as a trainer in 14 fights

"Couldn't be anything easier. When I win a fight, it's 'We won it.' When I lose a fight, I lost it."

Willie Pastrano, middleweight champ, on wanting to become a trainer after his boxing career

"Who did Angelo Dundee ever fight? Did Kevin Rooney ever hit anyone for me?"

Mike Tyson, on the importance of trainers

TRAINING SCHEDULE

"I like to have fun training, make my work my play."

Max Baer

"All his fine appearance was done by rubbing."

Phil Casey, trainer of John L. Sullivan, who rarely exercised

"Square that I was . . . I'd win a fight and the next day, I'd be back in the gym."

Ezzard Charles, on his devotion to training

"Not consciously."

> *Tex Cobb, asked if he had ever been*
> *in better shape than before facing*
> *Larry Holmes*

"Training fighters is like trying to catch a fish. It's technique, not strength."

> *Angelo Dundee*

"We go by Evander's grunts. The way he has been grunting the last couple of days, Bowe is in trouble."

> *Lou Duva, on Holyfield's training*
> *before his first fight with Riddick*
> *Bowe, which he lost*

"Depends on how far my refrigerator is."

> *George Foreman, asked how far he*
> *runs in practice*

"Sometimes you have to back off, so the fighter takes into the ring everything he's got and doesn't leave it in the gym or on the road."

> *Eddie Futch, on overtraining*

"Training promising kids is like putting a quarter in one pocket and taking a dollar out of another."
Charlie Goldman, Rocky Marciano's trainer

"Until the Lennox Lewis fight, I was what you would call a hip-hopping, hot-dogging, drinking, scheming, big-daddy son of a gun."
Oliver McCall, before beating Lennox Lewis for the title

"Old fighters react to training the way beautiful women react to scrubbing floors."
Norman Mailer

"I drink beer to help build up my stamina."
Leon Spinks

"Three six-packs a night."
Ron Standler, asked to describe his training regimen at the end of his career

"Work! Nobody ever said it was easy. . . . If it was fun, everybody would be doing it."

> *Ron Standler, on being forced to train aspiring boxers for a living*

"When you're training, you're free."

> *Mike Tyson, on problems outside of boxing*

"Even a chicken isn't afraid of Bramble."

> *David Wolf, Ray Mancini's manager, when told Livingstone Bramble trained with a chicken that refused to run around the ring*

TRUTH BE TOLD

"Yesterday I was lying. Today I'm telling the truth."

> *Bob Arum, after contradicting a statement he made a day earlier*

"I'm a nut on the truth bit."

> *Don King, on all the allegations against him*

"You can't believe anything anybody says in boxing."

Don King

"I don't want to tell you any half-truths unless they're completely accurate."

Dennis Rappaport, on rumors about Tommy Hearns's training sessions

MIKE TYSON

"Nothing is going to stop Tyson that doesn't have a motor attached."

David Brenner, on Mike Tyson's fighting Michael Spinks

"Just what I said I'd do: Whip his ass."

Buster Douglas, asked what he'd accomplished by what he did against Tyson in Japan

"The toughest man in the planet is afraid of a man who's older than dirt."

George Foreman

"He's not all that bad. If you dig deep—dig real deep, dig, dig, dig, dig, dig, deep, deep, go all the way to China—I'm sure you'll find there's a nice guy in there."

> *George Foreman, on Tyson*

"Tyson ain't no terror. He's really a pussycat. Give me two, three weeks from women and booze and I'd kick his butt. I'm serious."

> *Joe Frazier*

"Fighters, regardless of their talents, fight differently. They are intimidated by an aura of invincibility."

> *Jim Jacobs, on opponents' approaches to fighting Tyson*

"The only man who can beat Mike Tyson is Apollo Creed."

> *Sugar Ray Leonard*

"Sly Stallone's the only one I can figure, and only if he gets script rights."

> *Mike Littwin, sportswriter, asked who can beat Tyson*

"The only man Mike Tyson ever ducked was [commentator] Larry Merchant."

Allan Malamud, Los Angeles Times

"Does Mike Tyson live near here?"

Nelson Mandela, when asked, while walking through Manhattan, if he had any questions

"It was announced that Mike Tyson's next fight will be on regular television instead of pay-per-view. It will be on November 4 from 9:00 to 9:01."

Conan O'Brien, on the Mike Tyson–Buster Mathis Jr. fight

UGLY

"Too ugly to be champion."

Muhammad Ali, on Leon Spinks

"Holmes is so ugly, his grandmother said when he started to cry, the tears would stop and roll down the back of his head."

Muhammad Ali

THE VOODOO
THAT YOU DO

"Ray, tell me how your eyes feel. See how your eyes are jumping?"

> *Livingstone Bramble, after bringing*
> *in a voodoo doll and poking its eyes*
> *at the weigh-in before his second fight*
> *with Ray Mancini*

"He charges more for title fights."

> *Livingstone Bramble, on giving more*
> *money to his voodoo doctor after*
> *facing Ray Mancini for the*
> *lightweight title*

"He not only has to worry about my muscle, he has to fight my mind."

> *Lou Nova, heavyweight contender,*
> *describing the challenge faced by his*
> *opponent, Max Baer, after Nova*
> *hired a mystic to prepare for the fight*

MICKEY WALKER

"He didn't beat them all, but he beat most of them
and compiled probably one of the greatest records
ever for quantity and quality of men he fought."
Paul Gallico

WARTIME

"If America were in a just war, I'd volunteer for the
front line. I'd do the shuffling and win the war."
*Muhammad Ali, on his opposition to
the Vietnam War*

"It gives you direction and discipline, and I like the
picture of the guys in their hats and uniforms."
*Riddick Bowe, on his plans to join
the military after he retires*

"If I was a lieutenant, the boys might hesitate at
times to get close to me."
*Joe Louis, on refusing a promotion to
lieutenant during World War II and
instead remaining a sergeant*

"No, we'll win because we're on God's side."

> *Joe Louis, told that the Allies would win World War II because God was on our side*

"These are the types of muscles we're going to need to beat Germany with."

> *Franklin Delano Roosevelt, on Joe Louis's physique*

MIKE WEAVER

"There may have been a more obscure world heavyweight champion than Mike Weaver, but research has not yet unearthed his name."

> *Jack Fiske, sportswriter*

WEIGH-IN

"Love me. Love me not."

> *Max Baer, picking at Primo Carnera's chest hair before their weigh-in*

"That night I became the first fighter in history to be carried into the ring."

> *Art Aragon, on reducing to make the required weight cutoff*

"I don't know if I want to see Gregory that soon."

> *Riddick Bowe, on the possibility of fighting again in four months and facing the diet program that Dick Gregory put him on*

"I can't have my turkey and pumpkin pie. I've got to keep this slim, trim, schoolgirl figure."

> *Tex Cobb, asked if was planning to have a big Thanksgiving meal the day before his fight against Larry Holmes*

"A 255-pound semisolid tub of pudding."

> *Lowell Cohn, on Leroy Jones*

"I went to a basketball game one night and some people hollered at me. I thought they knew me. Not so. They thought I was Refrigerator Perry."

George Foreman, on reaching the 300-pound mark

"I eat what I eat and I weigh what I weigh."

George Foreman

"Why all the fuss? He's a heavyweight: ain't no weight to make."

Eddie Futch, on all the concern over Riddick Bowe's weight prior to a bout

"I've never seen a small person beat me at nothing."

Buster Mathis, asked if his 300 pounds were a disadvantage

"Tubbs probably doesn't want to be mistaken for a sumo wrestler."

Wallace Matthew, on Tony Tubbs's training with Lou Ferrigno

"You can eat anything you want, as long as you don't swallow it."

Archie Moore, discussing his new diet

"I have an advantage in this fight. I've only got one chin to expose."

Tommy Morrison, before fighting George Foreman

"When he turns sideways, he tends to disappear. If he ate a chicken, he'd bulge."

Jim Murray, on the skinny Tommy Hearns

"Buster Douglas entered the ring looking like something that should be floating over a Thanksgiving Day Parade."

Jim Murray, after Douglas faced Holyfield

"I don't have any three-piece suits. I always buy double-breasted jackets and hide my gut."

Rock Newman, on having to dress better after Riddick Bowe won the title

"He went to bed as a 231-pound champion and woke up as a 276-pound parade float."
Scott Ostler, on Buster Douglas

CHUCK WEPNER

"He moved around the ring as gracefully as a lump of mashed potatoes, and hit about as hard."
Michael Katz, on Chuck Wepner

WHEN IT ABSOLUTELY, POSITIVELY HAS TO BE THERE

"One of your trucks ran over my dog."
Mike Tyson, meeting Dave Raffo of UPI (an aide to Tyson later explained, "No, Mike, that was UPS")

WHITE HOPES

"We would draw so many WASPs that it would be a regulation beehive."

> *Tex Cobb, imagining facing Gerry*
> *Cooney for the heavyweight title*

WORKING STIFF

"It's just a job. Grass grows, birds fly, waves pound the sand. I beat people up."

> *Muhammad Ali*

"Did you know that my brother was a boxer? He used to box oranges."

> *Anonymous, old boxing joke*

"I like to feel I've earned my shower."

> *George Chuvalo, on being regarded*
> *as a hard worker in the ring*

"I don't really have a style. . . . I'm sort of on-the-job training."

Tex Cobb, on his fighting style

"I'm not standing up for the great state of Texas or the state of the white race or any of that. I'm a guy making a living."

Tex Cobb, on what he stands for in the ring

"All I want to do is hit somebody in the mouth. It's a whole lot easier than working for a living."

Tex Cobb

"We've all been blessed with God-given talents. Mine just happens to be beating people up."

Sugar Ray Leonard

"If fighters didn't get paid, if I had to take a job on the side, I'd still fight."

Floyd Patterson

"Coffee breaks and $200 a week for construction labor. Who needs to go into the ring?"

Charlie Rose, in 1962, on why there were no great fighters

"I don't love the fight game. It's just a means of getting security. You ever see a lion tamer who enjoys his job?"

Earnie Shavers

"You're lucky. You've never had to work for a living."

Emanuel Stewart, trainer, to Tommy Hearns

YOU CAN LOOK IT UP

"The greatest guy this country ever produced was Daniel Webster, the guy who wrote the dictionary."
John L. Sullivan

TONY ZALE

"It's always got to be some kind of a fight when guys like him and me fight, because there's only one way we can fight."

Rocky Graziano, on his legendary fights with Tony Zale

"Whenever Zale hits you in the belly, it's like someone stuck a hot poker in you and left it there."

Billy Soose

FRITZIE ZIVIC

"I learned more in 10 rounds than in all my other fights put together."

Sugar Ray Robinson, on fighting
Fritzie Zivic

INDEX

*An asterisk appears before names that
are referred to in a quote. All other
names are the actual sources of a quote.

235

242